BUMPER STICKER LIBERALISM

Peeling Back the Idiocies
of the Political Left

Mark Goldblatt

BROADSIDE BOOKS
An Imprint of HarperCollins*Publishers*
www.broadsidebooks.net

HarperCollins books may be purchased for educational, business, or sales promotional use. For information, please write: Special Markets Department, HarperCollins Publishers, 10 East 53rd Street, New York, NY 10022.

Broadside Books™ and the Broadside logo are trademarks of HarperCollins Publishers.

FIRST EDITION

Designed by Katy Riegel

Library of Congress Cataloging-in-Publication Data

Goldblatt, Mark.
Bumper sticker liberalism / Mark Goldblatt.—1st ed.
p.   cm.
Includes bibliographical references.
ISBN 978-0-06-213511-7
1. Liberalism—United States.   2. Bumper stickers.   I. Title.

JC574.2.U6G645   2012
320.51'30973—dc23
2012016498

12 13 14 15 16   OV/RRD   10 9 8 7 6 5 4 3 2 1

For

my mother,

Leona Goldblatt,

who would have been

antagonized by every page

Contents

Bumper Sticker Liberalism

Sticker Shock:
By Way of an Introduction

It's a runaway American dream, and you're right in the middle of it. You're cruising along Route 80 at fifty-five miles per hour, not a mile per hour more or less because that's the kind of law-abiding guy you are; you're taking in the sights: the purple mountains, the fruited plains, the billboard for the next Applebee's. You've got Springsteen songs blaring through the speakers—early Springsteen, before he got preachy, back when he was still crowbarring neighborhood girls' names into his lyrics in order to get laid. *This* is the reason you're here, moments like this, the reason your great-grandparents slept on roach-infested mattresses in the holes of steamships, the reason your grandparents worked seventy-five-hour weeks taking in laundry and digging ditches, the reason your mom made you do your homework in grammar school, the reason your dad enlisted to fight the Nazis; the generations have unwound themselves to this, to this life, to this American life, to this two-week paid vacation, to this instant, to you, your music, your tinted windshield, at one with the manifest destiny of the United States . . .

Then, at once, you hear a quick horn tap and notice, out of the corner of your eye, a silver blur veering out in front of you. You're being cut off . . . sideswiped if you don't react. You pump the brake and swerve to the right, avoiding the Prius by no more than a couple of feet. Your heart races, but you manage to control your vehicle, which now trails the Prius by several yards. You take a deep breath, then another. You stare out at the Prius, at the back of the driver's head, more in astonishment than in anger. Then, at last, you catch sight of his bumper sticker:

"Heal the Earth. Stop Making People."

If you were a road rage kind of guy, rather than a law-abiding kind of guy, you'd be ramming that sentiment right up Peter Prius's ass about now. But that's not you. What's more, you're as fond of the earth as the next terrestrial. You recycle. You turn off the light when you leave a room. You don't run the air conditioner when no one's home.

Except now the weenie in the weenie-mobile is telling you where to park your wiener? You wonder how that snide little dispatch from ecocentral is going to sit with your next-door neighbors who, after years of trying to start a family, just took out a second mortgage on their home to pay for in vitro fertilization. Who's going to tell them that their pursuit of happiness has to be canceled for the well-being of Gaia, that those baby booties the missus has been knitting carry too large a carbon footprint?

You wonder if such qualms have ever crossed the mind of Peter Prius, if he's thought past the slogan, if he has the vaguest inkling of the totalitarian overtones of *Stop Making People*.

Then again isn't that the point of a political bumper sticker? You don't have to think about it. You don't have to think *beyond* it. You don't have to think. It's the perfect antidote to critical thought. It's clever, pithy, often nasty . . . and altogether unexamined. It's an argumentative marker, a gauntlet thrown down from the sanctuary of the driver's seat. You don't have to defend your ideas with your pedal to the metal. Your bumper sticker says, in effect, "This is how I roll."

But it does more than that. It divvies up the world, separates the enlightened few from the benighted many, the courageous truth-tellers from the craven deniers, the wheat from the chaff; it *usses* in the us and *thems* out the them without slowing you down even one mile per hour. No back-sassing. No tailgating. No wind resistance.

Honk as you eat my self-righteous dust!

Which brings us to the title of this book: *Bumper Sticker Liberalism*. What I'm going to argue is that modern American liberalism is no longer a system of beliefs about the role of government, the conduct of international relations, or the nature of personal responsibility. Rather, it's a series of bumper stickers. Actual bumper stickers that signal mental bumper stickers. They don't make sense individually. They don't make sense in concert. Yet if you peel them away, one by one, from the foreheads of liberals, there's nothing left underneath.

It was not always thus. Enough has been written about the ironic evolution of the term *liberal*—the fact that many of today's conservative thinkers would have been classified, less than a century ago, as classical liberals in the tradition of John Locke, Adam Smith and Thomas Jefferson. So let's take the term as we find it . . . that is, a contemporary *liberal* is a person who believes that government should work toward leveling the material conditions of its citizens; that discrepancies in individual attainment, especially if they track with ethnic, gender, or sexual identities, must be the result of ongoing oppression; that intellectual, moral, or cultural judgments always reflect the bias of whoever is doing the judging; that the idea of objective truth or impartial standards is fraudulent, and that human beings occupy no special place in the grand scheme of things—indeed, that the very notion of a "grand scheme of things" is a quaint superstition. In other words, contemporary liberals prize equality—among people, among perspectives, even among biological species—over every other value. The lone hierarchy liberals will admit, the lone exception to their dogged egalitarianism, is their conviction that conservatives are always wrong.

There is nothing extraordinarily worrisome about any of this. The worry comes when liberals attempt to translate their egalitarian impulses into political action. For in doing so, they always get mugged by reality: *The real world is not an egalitarian place.* On the contrary, the real world is teeming with intellectual, moral and cultural hierarchies, self-evident truths and universal standards. To acknowledge these, for liberals, is to get caught up in the inexorable logic that leads to conservatism. It is argumentative suicide.

Thus the liberal bumper sticker.

★

THE ORIGINS OF the bumper sticker are murky. The automobile bumper came into widespread use in the United States with the introduction of the Ford Model A in 1927. It was intended as nothing more than a safety device. But the very nature of the thing—a metal attachment designed to get scuffed up, and thus unsuitable to inlaid ornamentation, yet always in the sight line of the driver behind you—cried out with commercial possibilities. The earliest bumper stickers weren't even "stickers"; they were cardboard and metal advertisements affixed with wire that was wrapped around the bumper. The first true bumper *sticker* seems to have been the brainchild of Forest P. Gill, a Kansas City silk screener and local businessman, who, in the years after World War II, utilized two new inventions: fluorescent Day-Glo ink and tough, adhesive-backed paper. The bumper sticker soon became a popular souvenir of life on the road, evidence of the worldly driver's encounters with various tourist traps, amusement parks and county fairs.[1]

The evolution of the bumper sticker from a miniature travelogue to an expression of personal and political belief picked up steam in the 1950s, with the Dwight Eisenhower–Adlai Stevenson presidential contests of 1952 and 1956: "I Like Ike" versus "Madly for Adlai." (Notice that conservatives, even then, preferred their rhymes straight; liberals, offbeat and slanty and nonjudgmental.) Like many things in America, the bumper sticker took an infantile turn in the second half of the 1960s with in-your-face mottos such as "Make Love, Not War" and "Black Power." Much has been written about that grotesquely celebrated era—I'll have more to say about it in the chapters that follow—but if you're looking for the moment when political bumper stickers mutated from happy declarations of candidate preferences to stand-alone rationales for collective action, this was it.

The title of this book, again, is *Bumper Sticker Liberalism*, and my intention is to show the inadequacy—as charitable a word as I can come up with—of left-of-center sloganeering on a number of fronts. The majority of these critiques, if you boil them down, carry the same message: Reality is more complex than many liberals want to believe or are willing to admit. That doesn't mean conservatives are guiltless in this regard; there is an undeniable bumper sticker mentality on the right, too. "Defend Your Constitution Before It's Too Weak to Defend You," for example, is no more thoughtful as a policy recommendation than "Tax Wealth— Not Work." In other words, it wouldn't be especially hard to write a book called *Bumper Sticker Conservatism* . . . but it wouldn't be nearly as much fun because conservatives, as a rule, don't have the same hyperinflated view of their own intellects as liberals do.

Indeed, as we'll discover, once you scratch through their egalitarian rhetoric, contemporary liberals often betray themselves as insufferable elitists. Elitism, to be sure, is as old as human society. But rarely has a less cerebrally, morally, or spiritually elite Elite looked down their collective nose at their countrymen. The minimum requirement for membership in the intelligentsia used to be, well, intelligence. This is no longer the case among liberals. Rather, what is now required is the mere sense of your own superiority, the smirky confidence that flows from a SparkNotes grasp of history, philosophy and literature, and which can be sustained only by a maniacal deafness to counterarguments. Listening to your political adversaries is deadly under such circumstances; they must therefore be dismissed, a priori, as stupid.

What's the matter with Kansas? liberals ask. The specific wording comes from a 2004 bestseller,[2] but it's a perennial liberal question, maybe *the* perennial liberal question, tinged with both condescension and exasperation: *Don't those working-class hicks who vote for conservative Republicans year after year realize that their economic interests lie with liberal Democrats?* Even if it were true—and it's not—that liberal policies served the economic interests of the working class, why should the working class cast their votes based strictly on their economic interests? Shouldn't they also take into consideration which party reflects their moral values? On the other hand, if economic interests trump all else, shouldn't every prosperous liberal vote a straight Republican ticket . . . since Republicans push for lower tax rates while Democrats seek to redistribute wealth? *Of course not,* liberals respond, *because we know the right thing to do.* Liberals, in short, take into account more than their narrow economic interests when they vote. It's a sign of their sophistication. They just don't expect conservatives to think that way.

The truth—and I say this having spent more than two decades writing newspaper and magazine columns for conservative readers, and having spent the majority of my waking hours surrounded by liberal colleagues, friends and lovers—is that there is an uncanny intellectual symmetry between the right and the left. Generally speaking, conservatives grasp this point and believe that liberals are merely wrong in their politics; liberals fail to grasp it and believe that conservatives are morons. But the symmetry remains. There are cartoonish extremes on both sides, to be sure. Even at the extremes, however, there is no discernible IQ gap between the rubes hopping around the Montana woods, sporting camouflage fatigues and toting copies of *The Turner Diaries* and the rubes bopping around the SoHo bar scene, sporting multiple piercings and toting copies of Chomsky's *9-11*. The two groups are, in fact, mirror images. Both grapple with ill-defined notions of autonomy and community, both are filled with rage at the government—which both view as malevolent and conspiratorial—and each group feels oppressed, in some distant but palpable way, by the other. The only significant difference is that the members of the SoHo crowd pay more for their clothes.

That's a cheap shot, I suppose.

Rest assured, more will follow.

1

═══★═══

Race to the Bottom

"All Republicans May Not Be Racist, But if You Are a Racist, You Are Probably a Republican"

The archetypal liberal is the kind of guy who, every morning, drops a dollar in the lap of the bum camped outside his apartment building and who, every evening, blames conservatives for the fact that there's a bum camped outside his apartment building. Liberals, in other words, don't think in terms of consequences. Short term. Long term. They don't like consequences. Consequences are annoying, messy and almost never exactly what you had in mind.

On the other hand, liberals *love* intentions. Especially good ones. As long as your intentions are good, you can do no wrong. This is the liberal gospel—or at least it would be the liberal gospel if the entire notion of a "gospel" didn't send liberals running for their finger quotes.

Nowhere is the liberal preference for intentions over consequences more evident than in their ongoing desperation to address . . . and address . . . and address the problem of race in America. You want to understand how liberals think about race? Rent *Precious*, the 2009 Oscar-nominated movie starring Gabourey Sidibe, Mo'Nique and Mariah Carey. *Precious* is a wet dream of progressive ideology, a deep-throated paean to the efficacy of good intentions. The title character, a bright young black woman with a heart of gold and the waistline of an asteroid, is driven to a grab bag of pathological behaviors by rotten environments at home and in her 'hood . . . until, at last, she's rescued from despair by community outreach and social programs. You know, the kind of stuff liberals have struggled to fund, over the objections of heartless bottom-line-minded conservatives, since the 1960s.

Phew, lucky thing "Each One Teach One" came along, or we might have the makings of a permanent black underclass!

Racial inequalities are real, of course—the legacy of America's sordid racial past, including centuries of slavery and legal segregation. You can make a reasonable case that the economic base of the country, dating back to colonial times, was built on the unrecompensed blood, sweat and tears of black slaves; southern slaveholders obviously profited from slave labor, but even Americans who didn't own slaves, even those who lived in northern states and territories where slavery was eventually abolished, profited from trade arrangements and business ventures made possible by dirt-cheap goods and services. Thus, if you were a New York City dressmaker, circa 1850, you owed your livelihood to slave labor as surely as a Mississippi cotton farmer did. So, too, did the employee who stitched your dresses, and the workers who forged the sewing needles, and the exporter who sold the dresses overseas, and the builders who put together the ship on which the dresses were carried, and the sailors who sailed on it, and the businessmen who insured it. So, too, did the descendants of those people, who lived comfortable and prosperous lives because of the hard work of their ancestors.

Taking that argument a step further, you can say that even those Americans who arrived *after* slavery was banned by the Thirteenth Amendment profited from slavery in the sense that they had access to economic opportunities rooted in pre–Civil War commerce.

Whether you buy into that narrative in its totality, or in part, or even just in granular form, it's hard to observe the socioeconomic struggles of the descendants of African slaves and not feel at least a twinge of guilt. For many liberals, that guilt is the epicenter of their political consciences. The fact that a disproportionate number of dark-skinned citizens continue to languish at the bottom rungs of American society is a call to action. The question is, once you've taken note of the problem, how do you remedy it?

The most straightforward solution would be direct financial reparations, the "forty acres and a mule" promised to former southern slaves in January 1865 by General William Tecumseh Sherman. Forty acres was considered, at the time, enough land to support a family farm—which the mule would be used to plow. But there are at least three major drawbacks to this approach: (1) providing forty acres and a mule, or the cash equivalent, to every descendant of an African slave would bankrupt the nation and thus render the wealth transfer worthless when the checks bounced; (2) many black Americans—President Obama, for example—would receive nothing since their ancestors were never enslaved, so the optics of a dark-skinned underclass would remain; (3) given the moral depravity of contemporary black culture, there is a strong likelihood that many young black men would immediately hock their forty acres to finance a hip-hop promotional company and trade their mule for an Xbox and a new set of rims.

Since direct cash reparations won't work, liberals are left with indirect forms of reparation. In other words, government programs. Affirmative action is one such program. Liberals love affirmative action, hold it tight to their bosom, measure their moral worth by their commitment to it. Only an unrepentant racist, liberals tell themselves, could oppose affirmative action for black college applicants. The notion that affirmative action channels black students into educational environments for which they're unprepared, that it forces them to overload their schedules with tutoring and remedial courses, that it results in significantly lower grade point averages and significantly higher dropout rates is background noise to liberals—like the *wanh-wanh-wanh* sounds that substitute for adult voices in *Peanuts* cartoons. Liberals hear only that conservatives don't want Jamal to get into Harvard, that they'd rather he go to some hellhole of a state school, which is where he'd be ticketed, based on his SAT scores, if not for the noble intentions of liberals. Conservatives don't want to cut Jamal a break . . . and for God's sake haven't his people suffered enough? Consequences, shmonsequences. For liberals, the movie ends as Jamal checks into his dorm room at Hollis Hall, hangs a poster of Martin Luther King above his desk, then glances out the window and sees the statue of John Harvard across the Old Yard. Cue the inspirational music. Now, quick, roll the closing credits.

The cameras are gone by the time Jamal, who tested a hundred points or so below his new white and Asian classmates in reading, writing and math skills, fails his first set of exams. The cameras are *long* gone when he's put on academic probation after his first semester. The cameras are a distant memory when he's handed an academic dismissal at the end of his first year.

Hey, at least Jamal was spared the indignity of doing his coursework at a second-tier college . . . where his standardized test scores indicated he belonged, and where he'd have had a greater chance to succeed. But now we're talking about consequences, and who cares about consequences? Harvard *needs* Jamal. It needs him for the sake of diversity. It needs him in order to look more like America . . . and we *all* need Harvard to look more like America, don't we?[1] That's the intention of affirmative action, to make Harvard look more like America. That's the intention of its liberal advocates. How else are we going to heal our racial wounds? Given that intention, how dare conservative critics question affirmative action?

News flash: The fact that you oppose big government programs designed to help black people does not mean you oppose helping black people. *Big government programs often don't work.* Except when I say they "often don't work," what I mean is they "hardly ever work" . . . unless you define "working" as "making liberals feel good about themselves," in which case big government programs almost always work exactly as intended, even as they're screwing over the very populations they were designed to help. Thus a 2004 study by the *Stanford Law Review*[2] showed that affirmative action in law school admissions had resulted in significantly *fewer* black lawyers actually practicing in the United States.

The most tragic instance of this, of course, came with the expansion of Aid to Families with Dependent Children. (You might recognize it by the more generic term, *welfare*, or by the name of the program that superseded it in 1997, Temporary Assistance for Needy Families, or TANF.) AFDC dates back to the Franklin Roosevelt administration and the Great Depression. The program was initially designed to assist impoverished widows and their children. But its scope was broadened during the 1960s, as part of Lyndon Johnson's Great Society, to include payments to unmarried mothers living with children. Why? Because the out-of-wedlock birthrate among blacks in 1963 stood at a record high of 23.6 percent. Thus many single black mothers who were struggling to support their families were ineligible for assistance under the old AFDC rules. How could liberals sit by and watch their hardships? How could they do nothing? So AFDC was expanded to include unwed mothers.

The government began, in effect, to sponsor illegitimacy.

As of this writing, more than four decades removed from the expansion of AFDC benefits, the out-of-wedlock birthrate among blacks has tripled to 70 percent. Now ask yourself: Is there any social pathology known to man not found disproportionately among children raised by single parents? (Answer: no.) With only the most noble of intentions, in short, liberals did more to undermine the structural integrity of the black family than did decades of Jim Crow laws, eventually spawning a wildly degenerate urban culture in which the phrase "baby daddy" came to eclipse "husband."

LBJ's Great Society fiasco inaugurated the era of white-liberal-guilt politics, sponsored by what Saul Bellow once called "the Good Intentions Paving Company," whose distorting consequences have reverberated ever since. The 1970s brought forced busing in an effort to integrate underperforming, predominantly black inner-city schools. This ignited white flight to the suburbs, which further segregated public schools, eroded local tax bases and thus cut funds for the very school systems busing was intended to help.

Next came affirmative action—which, besides consigning underprepared black students to bottomed-out grade point averages and higher dropout rates also stigmatized the achievements of black students admitted on their own merits. You often hear echoes of this when liberals criticize black conservatives: *Well, you know, he only got where he is today because of affirmative action, so isn't he a big old hypocrite for opposing it now?* Liberals assume, in other words, that successful blacks owe their success to the good intentions of liberals. Isn't that belief, in itself, racist?

The question returns us to the bumper sticker notion that if you're a racist, you're likely a Republican. It depends on how racism is defined. If we define racism in the broadest and simplest sense possible, as a visceral dislike of people who don't look like you, and if we further limit our discussion only to party affiliation . . . even then, it's questionable whether more Republicans than Democrats would qualify as racist. Statistics of this sort are hard to come by, naturally. But we do know that black people are overwhelmingly Democratic by party affiliation, and, according to at least four separate studies, roughly four times more likely than whites to hold anti-Semitic views.[3] Anecdotally, we notice persistent anti-white and anti-Asian sentiments expressed by blacks; anti-black sentiments expressed by Asians; anti-black and anti-Asian sentiments expressed by Hispanics. Each of these minorities is a solid Democratic voting bloc. Factor in another reliable Democratic constituency, labor unions, whose rank and file are hardly strangers to anti-immigrant rhetoric, and . . . well, you get the picture.

But of course we're still talking about the narrow issue of visceral racism and party affiliation. The more intriguing issue is how racism plays itself out in ideology. Is conservatism inherently more racist than liberalism? Again, the answer depends on what constitutes racism. If, for example, your definition of a racist is anyone who doesn't like big government programs meant to equalize outcomes across racial identities, then, yeah, conservatives are more likely to be racists than liberals because conservatives, as a rule, don't like big government programs. If, on the other hand, your definition of a racist is anyone who believes that black people cannot be held to the same intellectual and moral standards as nonblacks, that the only way to equalize outcomes across racial identities is for the government to step in and put its big, fat thumb on the scales, then liberals are *far* more likely to be racists than conservatives.

Still, liberals *mean* well. They always mean well. If you think that the Good Intentions Paving Company has laid its last stretch of road, take a moment to consider the ongoing repercussions of the Community Reinvestment Act. Signed into law by Jimmy Carter in 1977, the CRA inaugurated a concerted, decades-long effort by the federal government to coerce banks into making home loans to lower-income borrowers. Again, the intention was noble—though rooted, as usual, in a desperate race consciousness. If more black families owned their own homes, the theory went, they'd accumulate wealth as the properties increased in value. They'd eventually pass that wealth down to their children, and the financial inequalities stemming from America's past racial sins would gradually diminish.

The altogether foreseeable problem is that mathematical probabilities don't bend to noble intentions. The reason that banks weren't lending to black borrowers as frequently, or on as good terms, as to white borrowers had nothing to do with racism. It had to do with risk analysis. Writing loans to lower-income, lower-collateral borrowers inevitably means more defaults. Hence, the designation: *subprime loans.*

But liberals (and, to be fair, more than a few "compassionate" conservatives) wanted black families to own their homes, and, with the passage of the CRA, the Carter administration started turning up the heat on banks to make it happen. With the rise of subprime lending, banks were able to offset the increased risk by charging escalating interest rates. The feds nodded approvingly. To further grease the skids, banks were encouraged to reformulate and repackage the riskier loans, share their exposure and tap into other sources of revenue. Congress helped out with various forms of deregulation.[4] The price of real estate soared because of new demand from those who would otherwise have been unable to buy a house. Speculators soon moved in because there seemed no way to lose . . . and then, well, you know the rest. The mortgage meltdown of 2008, grotesque foreclosure rates, a deep global recession and a credit crunch.

Sooner or later, mathematical probabilities have their way.

The bitterest irony, though also the most predictable, is that a disproportionate number of foreclosures affected black homeowners since they were riskier buyers to begin with.

Driving past all those houses with moving-sale furniture scattered across the front lawns, liberals could at least take comfort in knowing their hearts were in the right place.

"Celebrate Black History"

On July 16, 2009, police officers in Cambridge, Massachusetts, responded to a 911 call from a woman named Lucia Whalen. Whalen had observed two men in the act of breaking into her neighbor's home in a ritzy section of town. The police showed up minutes later, climbed onto the porch and noticed two dark-skinned men inside the house. Sergeant James Crowley of the Cambridge Police Department knocked on the door. One of the men inside, Henry Louis Gates, a Harvard professor and perhaps the most distinguished black scholar in the United States, came to the front door. Crowley didn't recognize Gates; he also didn't know that Gates rented the house from the university or that Gates and his "usual driver"—the second man—had had trouble with a faulty lock on the front door. Gates asked Crowley what the problem was, and Crowley explained that he was responding to a report of a possible break-in; he asked Gates to step out onto the porch. Gates told him that he was a Harvard professor and the legal resident of the house but refused to come out onto the porch. Crowley then asked Gates if he could prove it. Gates said he could, and he led Crowley back into the kitchen. There, Gates produced proper ID, and he asked Crowley for his name and badge number.

That much is undisputed in Gates's own recollection of the event[5] and in the official police report.[6] But the accounts differ in other ways. Crowley claims Gates injected the element of race at the start, answering Crowley's initial request to come outside with "Why, because I'm a black man in America?" Gates claims Crowley wouldn't provide his name or badge number; Crowley insists that Gates became more and more belligerent as he tried to leave the house, with Gates telling him at one point that he had "no idea who he was messing with." Both sides agree that Crowley asked Gates if he wanted to continue their discussion on the porch; according to Crowley, Gates replied, "I'll speak with your mama outside." Gates denies he said this—though police recordings reveal an enraged male voice yelling something inaudible in the background—but he did eventually follow Crowley onto the porch, at which point Crowley arrested Gates for disorderly conduct. After he was put in handcuffs, by his own account, Gates asked, "Is this how you treat a black man in America?"

Gates was charged with disorderly conduct and released after four hours in police custody. The charge was dropped five days later. The entire business might have been forgotten except that on July 22—six days after Lucia Whalen made her fateful 911 call—President Obama was asked to comment on the incident during a news conference. Though conceding he didn't know all the facts, Obama stated that the police had "acted stupidly in arresting somebody when there was already proof that they were in their own home." After a wave of criticism from law enforcement officials nationwide, Obama backtracked a bit, saying that he "could have calibrated those words differently."[7] He invited both men to the White House for a beer with him and Vice President Biden—a photo op that became known as the Beer Summit—and echoed other commentators who suggested that incident could serve as a "teachable moment."[8]

The confrontation between Officer Crowley and Professor Gates is indeed a "teachable moment"—though not in the way President Obama intended. The main lesson to be drawn from it has nothing to do with racial profiling, or with police attitudes toward minority suspects, or, more broadly, with alleged biases in the criminal justice system. These, of course, are the familiar lessons taught on a continual basis, with or without "moments," by knee-jerk liberal educators across the country.

The true lesson of the Crowley-Gates affair is that even a tenured Ivy League professor who commands a high six-figure salary for negligible classroom work, a public intellectual who hosts taxpayer-supported TV series, jetting off to Africa[9] and China[10] to do research and then getting chauffeured back to his house, a bestselling author honored from coast to coast and toasted on both sides of the Atlantic, *even Skip Gates* has bought hook, line and sinker into the myth of perpetual white conspiracies against blacks.

I don't mean this as a personal indictment of Gates—whom I've met several times and who has always struck me as a genuinely good guy. I mean it as a criticism of a generic mind-set. Gates's former colleague at Harvard, Cornel West, coined the term *niggerization* to describe the systematic debasing and dehumanizing of black people in American culture.[11] Unlike Gates, who's the real deal as an intellectual, West is more of a polysyllabic dancing bear. But *niggerization* is a useful term. The belief that niggerization is an ongoing process is the only thing that unites the majority of black people in the twenty-first century; they are no longer bound by social or economic interests, by educational or occupational restrictions, by common experience or even common ancestry. Their connection to one another is now purely psychic: the unwavering conviction that every hiccup on their life's journey, every unrealized opportunity and unraveling ambition is due to racism. "There's a sense of malevolent ghosts darting around you, screwing with you, often out of sight but never out of mind," observes the critic Touré.[12] But what if there are no actual ghosts? What if the only thing screwing with you is your imagination?

Under the circumstances, trying to tell a black person that he is no longer a victim is like trying to tell him that he's no longer black.

Black victimhood has become black identity.

Even a sentiment as benign as the bumper sticker exhortation to "celebrate black history" hinges on that sense of perpetual victimhood. (Let's set aside, for the moment, the idea that history should be *celebrated* rather than merely studied and analyzed.) Because if we define history as a record of military conflict, scientific advance, social evolution, speculative thought and artistic endeavor—and, really, what's the alternative to that definition?—there's not very much black history to celebrate. The comparative meagerness of that record must thus be accounted for by reference to black victimhood.

Certainly, no one has done more over the last half century to "celebrate black history" than Henry Louis Gates. Besides authoring and editing enough popular and scholarly books of the black experience to stock a long library shelf, Gates scripted and hosted a six-part 1999 PBS series called *Wonders of the African World*, in which he set out to rediscover the glories of sub-Saharan African civilization. Those glories, however, proved elusive. Gates's own sense of disappointment becomes more and more palpable as each hour-long episode unwinds; around episode five, you can almost hear Peggy Lee singing in the background, "Is That All There Is?" But wait! Near the end of the final installment, episode six, Gates pays a visit to Great Zimbabwe, the capital of the kingdom of Zimbabwe, which dominated southern Africa from roughly AD 1300 to 1450. "I love this place," Gates declares, strolling among the uneven stone walls and broken footpaths. "There's nothing in sub-Saharan Africa quite like Old Zimbabwe." Looking straight into the camera, he adds, "When white explorers first stumbled across this incredible city in 1871, they were unwilling to believe that Africans could have built anything this grand."

Turning another corner as the camera pans up another eight-foot wall, Gates gushes, "It's extraordinary how they used the rocks to build the walls . . . it's brilliant!"

The climax of the episode, indeed of the entire series, comes moments later when Gates crosses paths with three visitors: two young women and a young man. The young man is a local tour guide; one of the young women is a native African. But Gates's attention is quickly drawn to the third visitor, a young woman who mentions that she's originally from New York City and is currently "an educator in Michigan." He asks her how she feels, strolling among these ruins. She is beaming with pride as she answers, "I think it's wonderful. It shows the *genius* of our people."

"Yeah, it does," Gates says.

Well, not quite.

What it shows, if we're going to be honest, is that sub-Saharan Africans were constructing thick stone walls around the time the French were topping off Notre Dame Cathedral in Paris. Such comparisons are the last thing on Gates's mind, however, as he smiles at the young woman and informs her, "Europeans kept coming up with theories saying Africans couldn't have built this. Did you know that?"

To which she rolls her eyes knowingly and says only, "Interesting . . ."

The notion that the stone walls of Zimbabwe show the "genius" of the people who inhabited the city is, in reality, the less significant error under which the young woman is laboring. The more significant error is that she has some special bond with sub-Saharan Africa because one or more of her remote ancestors lived there. Not only are Old Zimbabwe's stone walls nothing to write home about, but the people who built them aren't *her* people. The people of Old Zimbabwe are a curiosity, a minor slide in a PowerPoint lecture on forgotten civilizations. They're a people of a distant land and bygone time whose scant accomplishments she's been conditioned to magnify by *celebrations* of black history. Her *people*, if the term even has a coherent meaning, are from New York. Gates's *people* are from West Virginia. Old Zimbabwe might as well be a way station on the dark side of the moon.

But there's the rub—for the young woman, for Gates and for many, if not most, black Americans. Once you let go of the fantasy of bygone African glories, and the mystical connection to said glories that binds together black people everywhere, what remains of black identity except that sense of "niggerization" described by Cornel West? And even *that* is harder and harder to sustain when you wake up every morning and the president of the United States is a guy named Barack Hussein Obama.

The Obama presidency has, if anything, intensified the Quest for the Great White Sheet—that secret memorandum, or encrypted file, or videotaped handshake, or wink-and-nod gentlemen's agreement that every right-thinking (which is to say, left-thinking) black person knows is floating around somewhere out there in the American ether, engulfing him, holding him back, keeping him marginalized, blackballing him from the good life to which he is entitled, no matter how many bad choices he's made, no matter how many ways he's let down himself and the people around him, based on the injustices his ancestors suffered, even if his ancestors arrived in the United States too late to suffer them.

The old racial taboo used to be the word *nigger*. The one time I ever spoke the word as I child, repeating something a neighborhood boy had said, I couldn't get both syllables out; my mother slapped me in face between the two *g*'s. That taboo is long gone. If it weren't, there wouldn't be a seventy-five-foot billboard in Times Square of Sean P. Puff Diddy Daddy Combs, raising his fist in the iconic black power salute of the late 1960s—since Combs, after all, helped turn the word *nigger* into a hip-hop cottage industry and thus ensured that a generation of civil rights heroines like Rosa Parks and Coretta Scott King spent the last two decades of their lives bombarded by it. The new racial taboo isn't a word but an idea, a creeping suspicion that maybe the socioeconomic stagnation of black Americans is their own fault, that maybe the across-the-board statistical disparities between black Americans and every other ethnic group has less to do with the real sins of America's collective past than with individual human beings' failure to defer gratification. What is the new racial taboo? It's the acknowledgment that if institutional racism is defined as a concerted effort to deprive black people of their human and civil rights, it no longer exists. There, I've said it. My mother's dead, and I've said it: Institutional racism no longer exists. Let me italicize it: *Institutional racism no longer exists.* Let me set it apart, a paragraph unto itself:

Institutional racism no longer exists.

But if that's true, then are black Americans still black Americans? Or are they just Americans with darker than average skin?

"I'm Black and I'm Proud. I'm Black and I'm Proud. I'm Black and I'm Proud."

Racial essentialism is the belief that every member of a race possesses certain characteristics that every other member of that race also possesses. Essentialist reasoning and rhetoric have pock-marked American race relations since colonial times. Slavery itself was most often justified on essentialist grounds; Africans and their descendants, the institution's defenders claimed, were naturally suited to servitude. Essentialism did not diminish with the abolition of slavery. The notorious Racial Integrity Act, passed by the Virginia legislature in 1924, enshrined the "one-drop rule," which held that if even one of your ancestors was black, you necessarily had black blood coursing through your veins and thus counted as "colored."[13] The one-drop rule was a textbook case of essentialist politics, a desperate attempt to maintain hard and fast racial categories in a rapidly changing society—a society in which such categories were destined to be destabilized by integration, mixed marriages and biracial children.[14]

The failure of racial essentialism, however, stems not from its immoral uses but from its false premises. The concept of race, for all its cultural power, has always been a biological fiction. Variations among human populations are subtle and continuous across the entire planet. The color-coded dividing lines dreamed up in the eighteenth century by European thinkers like Carl Linnaeus (1707–78) and Johann Friedrich Blumenbach (1752–1840) do not correspond with real fault lines in the species.

Linnaeus, for example, first imagined four races: white Europeans, black Africans, red (native) Americans and brown Asians;[15] later, he adjusted the hue knob on Asians from brown to yellow and added a fifth catchall category, which he called *Monstrosities*, to cover "abnormal" specimens whom he couldn't shoehorn into one of the original four groupings. Beyond skin-deep descriptions, however, Linnaeus also observed a set of typical personality traits for each race. He perceived Europeans (surprise!) as gentle and intelligent; by contrast, American Indians were quick-tempered and stubborn, Africans lazy and negligent, Asians melancholy and severe, etc.[16]

Blumenbach began with five races, based upon his study of human skulls: white Caucasians, black Ethiopians, copper Americans, brown Malays and yellow Mongolians.[17] His racial descriptions are littered with decidedly unscientific qualifiers like "generally," "more or less" and "for the most part." He also notes that "each of the five principal races contains besides [as well] one or more nations which are distinguished by their more or less striking structure from the rest of those in the same division."[18] In other words, Blumenbach dodged Linnaeus's monstrous catch-all by admitting he'd included in each racial category groups of people who didn't quite fit.

To glimpse the futility of racial categorizations, here's a thought experiment: Imagine every adult male human being on the planet lined up in size places—with the shortest dwarf on the far left and the tallest giant on the far right. Now divide the line in half at five feet, nine inches. If you're five-nine or above, you're tall; if you're below five-nine, you're short. Got it? Now send everyone home. You're left with two groupings; let's call them "Talls" and "Shorts." Walking down the street, you can usually tell whether a guy is a Tall or a Short. After a while, the categories even start to feel natural. But they're not. There was no special reason to make the cut at five-nine. You could've made it at five-seven or five-eleven. Indeed, you could've made *two* cuts and wound up with three categories: Talls, Mediums and Shorts. Or you could've made four cuts and wound up with five categories: Very Talls, Talls, Mediums, Shorts and Very Shorts. There was no science involved. How many cuts you made, and where you made them, were always arbitrary.

But what if the Talls and the Shorts *themselves* bought into the groupings? The Talls, after all, know they're tall. They start to feel pretty good about themselves compared with the Shorts. The Shorts sense this and start to resent the Talls: *Those damn Talls are always lording it over us Shorts! They have no idea what it means to be Short! But we Shorts, we know what second-class citizenship feels like! We can see the pain in one another's eyes. That's our natural connection to one another. That's the tie that binds.*

But *is* there a natural connection among the Shorts? Does a guy who's five-eight have more in common, height-wise, with a guy who's five-ten or with a guy who's three-foot-nine? The answer is obvious. Five-eight has more in common with five-ten than with three-nine . . . unless, of course, the five-eight guy is so used to thinking of himself as a Short that he feels like a vertical sellout for acknowledging his connection with a Tall. No matter how tall he acts, his fellow Shorts tell him, the Talls will never accept him. He'll never be truly Tall. Even if he buys lifts for his shoes, he'll always be Short on the inside.

From a biological standpoint, categorizing human beings according to skin color or hair texture or facial features or skull shapes, or some combination of such factors, makes about as much sense as categorizing them according to height. The dividing lines are always arbitrary. Yet many otherwise intelligent people still insist that groupings like "black" and "white" and "brown" and "yellow" carry a deep truth, that every member of the group shares a mysterious blood-bond with every other member—and, in the case of black people, a mysterious spiritual link to a long-forgotten land that once upon a time was inhabited by at least one ancestor. Except this is nonsense on stilts. Henry Louis Gates, Derek Jeter and Mariah Carey each meet the essentialist, one-drop rule definition of a black person. But, apart from their no-man-is-an-island common humanity, do they *really* have much of a connection to one another?

Racial essentialism has waned, at least to a certain degree, since the end of the Jim Crow era. Sure, the national census still asks us to categorize ourselves by race, but the 2010 version provided us with fifteen races to choose from, left open the option of checking off more than one . . . and even invited us to make up our own classification if none of the above satisfied our self-image. But hard-core racial essentialism, like many other nutty ideas, continues to thrive in the only precinct in American life sufficiently divorced from reality to sustain it: academia. It is there, on college campuses across the United States, that we find the last great monument to racial essentialism: black studies.

To say that black studies should not exist is too harsh. Even if race is a make-believe anthropological category, the *concept* of race has exerted a profound and lasting influence on the history and culture of America—and, through America, the entire world. Studying the effects of racial consciousness could, in theory, be a valuable intellectual exercise. In practice, however, the "discipline" of black studies has had much more to do with cheerleading for blackness than with studying anything. Black studies exists for one reason: to instill in black students a sense of pride at the accomplishments of their African ancestors. Whether such pride is useful from a pedagogic standpoint, or justified from a factual standpoint, or even desirable from a deadly sin standpoint, is beside the point. The desperation of black studies professors to talk up the glories of precolonial Africa, and the desperation of black students to feel proud of their African roots, is akin to the desperation of Dorothy to return to Kansas in *The Wizard of Oz*: *There's no place like home. There's no place like home. There's no place like home.*

"I'm Black and I'm Proud. I'm Black and I'm Proud. I'm Black and I'm Proud."

This has been true from its very inception. There would be no such thing as black studies if cowardly white academics hadn't caved to student demands in the late 1960s to make college curricula more "relevant" and "inclusive." One of the first beneficiaries of that capitulation was Leonard Jeffries, a well-traveled bumpkin with an in-demand complexion. Jeffries, who founded and chaired the Black Studies Department at San José State College in the early 1970s before being granted instant tenure and installed as chairman of City College of New York's new African American Studies Department, was the essentialist's essentialist. He divided the human race into two groups: "sun people" (roughly equivalent to black people) and "ice people" (roughly equivalent to white people). Sun people, according to Jeffries, are "the African family of warm communal hope," peace-loving and compassionate; ice people, by contrast, are "the cold rigid element in world history,"[19] oppressive and competitive. Melanin—skin color—is what accounts for the difference in temperament. Blacks have more of it, which allows them to "negotiate the vibrations of the universe and to deal with the ultraviolet rays of the sun."[20]

To call this idiotic is to insult the thoughtfulness of idiots. But, in his own deluded way, Jeffries was sounding an early keynote in the intellectual pep rally that became black studies. His sun people—ice people dichotomy at least allowed him to account for the observable backwardness of sub-Saharan African civilization. Black people were just too damn peaceful and trusting to defend themselves against the devilish onslaught of whites—which was the only reason whites were able to conquer and exploit the grand and powerful black kingdoms of the past.

What kingdoms those were! Two thousand years before the Wright Brothers, black Africans were experimenting with aviation and aeronautics. They invented telescopes around the same time and happily sailed across the Atlantic for peaceful cultural exchanges with pre-Columbian Indians. They knew of quantum mechanics and gravitational theory . . . and, by the way, they were telepathic. Aristotle stole everything he wrote from the library of Alexandria in ancient Egypt, which was a pretty neat trick since the library was founded after he died. Oh, and the Egyptians themselves were black . . . which we'd all realize if centuries of white scholars hadn't concealed that fact from us.[21]

All of the above has been taught, based on information in assigned textbooks, in an accredited black studies program. Of course, it's unfair to tar the entire field with the sins of its worst practitioners. Black studies is dotted with respectable scholars—Gates is one of them—whose research happens to focus on the history of dark-skinned peoples. But the primary mission of such programs nationwide continues to be pumping up the self-esteem of black students rather than pursuing and promulgating truth. The folly of such a mission is compounded by the fact that study after study has indicated little or no correlation between self-esteem and positive life outcomes.[22] In other words, the social engineering component of black studies is as dubious as much of the scholarship.

Even worse, black studies has provided the pretext for a kinder, gentler form of segregation on college campuses. Many larger universities now offer minority students the opportunity to sign up for housing according to their ethnicity—with dormitories devoted not only to black cultural themes but also to Hispanic and Asian experiences.[23] Such dorms coordinate their "enrichment" activities with the corresponding ethnic studies departments on campus, thus reinforcing a sense of isolation and alienation from the larger community.

So, too, black student associations, which arose in conjunction with black studies departments in the late 1960s, continue the drumbeat of existential Otherness to which their members are subjected. It is a drumbeat that often starts the moment they arrive as freshmen and attend a "black student orientation" and lasts even after graduation when they are invited to join a "black alumni association."[24]

Such is the legacy of racial essentialism. It should not engender pride in anyone.

2

Dogma and Denial

**"If You Are Not an Environmentalist,
You Are Suicidal and Should Seek Therapy . . ."**

If you're writing up a checklist of the deadliest isms of the twentieth century, first place is a gimme. You can pencil in *communism* at the top position, then trace the letters in ink, then trace them again in a blood. Under Mao Tse-tung in China, the communist government rang up a body count estimated between twenty and forty million as a result of its Great Leap Forward, from 1958 to 1962. Mao took his inspiration from his fellow communist Joseph Stalin in the Soviet Union, who had manufactured twenty million corpses in the name of socioeconomic uniformity a quarter century earlier. You can heap onto the pile another two million victims of the communist Khmer Rouge regime under Pol Pot from 1975 to 1979—almost a quarter of the total population of Cambodia. Kim Il Sung in North Korea, Ho Chi Minh in Vietnam and

Fidel Castro in Cuba are pikers by comparison, but we shouldn't omit their contributions to the roll call of communist infamies.

Second place on your checklist is pretty clear cut, too: Nazism. Under Adolf Hitler from 1938 to 1945, Nazi Germany systematically exterminated eleven million civilians—including homosexuals, Slavs and the overwhelming majority of its own and neighboring Jewish populations. (The figure doesn't count battlefield casualties that can be laid at Hitler's doorstep.) Nazi victims don't stack up to communist victims in raw numerical terms, but the Nazis can claim the distinction of history's most mechanized and efficient genocide.

Third place is less certain. Fascism is a contender, but it's hard to distinguish from its übercentralized cousins, communism and Nazism. If you polled faculty lounges across the United States— and no one deserves a good hard polling more than university professors—capitalism might slide in here. It's true that twentieth-century capitalism produced pizza with extra cheese baked into the crust, which has greased the skids to an early grave for many a glutton, but the mechanisms of capitalism also defeated both Nazism and communism, and capitalist economies have done more to alleviate human suffering worldwide than any other force, so the aggregate case for ranking it among the deadliest isms is weak. Islamism is an up-and-comer, and it might contend in the twenty-first century, but its rise came too late to place it among the top-tier killer ideologies of the 1900s.

But what about *environmentalism*?

The 1962 publication of *Silent Spring* by Rachel Carson is often cited as the moment environmentalism went mainstream. By the second half of the decade the book had spawned a full-fledged, face-painting, tambourine-slapping movement, symbolized in our collective mental newsreel by the first Earth Day celebration in April 1970. The problem was that Carson's jeremiad about the effects of synthetic chemicals on the ecosystem was based on—to be as generous as possible—shaky evidence and dubious methodology.[1] But that was no concern to the flower children who got wind of Carson's thesis. They took her message to heart, and with their signature combination of ill-informed commitment, sanctimonious indignation and (as Yeats might have put it) passionate intensity, helped pressure the newly formed Environmental Protection Agency into banning Carson's personal hobgoblin, the pesticide DDT.

No matter that DDT had a track record of safe and effective use dating back to World War II, during which it was often applied directly to the skin of American soldiers.[2] Much of the developed world followed the American ban on DDT. That was great news if you were a buzzing insect. But it was exceptionally bad news if you were a human being living in sub-Saharan Africa—where mosquito-borne malaria continued to decimate vast populations.

Cut to 2006, more than three decades after the pesticide had been pointlessly phased out: The World Health Organization recommended the resumption of DDT use in malaria-ravaged areas, and the United States Agency for International Development announced that it would fund the effort. The cost of the DDT ban, in human lives, is difficult to calculate with accuracy. But it is certainly in the millions, perhaps in the tens of millions.[3]

More than enough to slot environmentalism in the top three killer ideologies of the twentieth century.

The DDT fiasco should serve as a cautionary tale for today's greener-than-thou liberals who demand drastic government action to curb the evil of global warming. But it doesn't give them pause, of course, because liberals of all stripes are more concerned with intentions than with consequences. Intentions don't get any nobler than saving the planet and ensuring a livable habitat for future generations. Which is why twenty-first-century environmentalists regard skeptics of global warming with roughly the same patience and forbearance that seventeenth-century Puritans regarded witches in Salem. They'd burn them in public if not for the greenhouse gases emitted by the fires.

Do global warming skeptics—the preferred liberal term is *deniers*—have a point? It's hard to make that call without an advanced degree in climatology. That said, there's an undeniable consensus among international scientific organizations and climatologists that global warming is real and scary. (Much like there was an undeniable consensus among international intelligence agencies and operatives that Iraq possessed stockpiles of weapons of mass destruction in 2003.) Yet the checkered, inadvertently genocidal track record of environmental alarmists is an altogether rational concern. The road-righteous suggestion that dissent from the prevailing green orthodoxy is "suicidal" and requires "therapy" is itself evidence of a cognitive impairment, akin to the compulsive gambler who doubles down on a so-so hand. *Maybe if I keep raising the stakes, these hellish uncertainties will go away.*

But what's the human cost of another enviro-*oops*?

Then, too, there's the counterevidence—the inherent dangers of groupthink, the fact that warming trends are irregular, the fact that half a century ago scientists were more worried about global cooling than about global warming, etc. Much of it, perhaps, can be explained away by experts. But certain observations can be made, even by a layperson, that should chasten us before we go legislating ourselves over a cliff.

The first such observation harks back to high school earth science. The earth has undergone several ice ages, which means that from time to time it cools down and then warms up on its own, with no input whatsoever from mankind. So when climatologists point out that recent warming trends have corresponded with increased carbon emissions by human beings, are they looking at a *cause* or merely a *correlation*?

The response to such a question is inevitably a blur of climatological data. So, for example, we are told that in 2009 the average concentration of carbon dioxide in the earth's atmosphere was 387 parts per million by volume (ppmv)[4]—the highest concentration, according to climatologists, in at least fifteen to twenty million years.[5] Human beings have been pumping out CO_2 emissions in greater and greater quantities ever since the Industrial Revolution, so no wonder the atmosphere is now saturated with the stuff.

Case closed, right?

Except if CO_2 concentration is at its highest level in fifteen to twenty million years, doesn't that mean that twenty million years ago, long before man got busy fouling the ecosystem with his ancient marshmallow roasts, the CO_2 level was higher than today? As a matter of fact, wasn't the level over 500 ppmv back then?[6] Oh, and if you go back sixty million years, wasn't the CO_2 concentration in the earth's atmosphere 2,000 ppmv—*more than five times higher than it is now*? That's an awful lot of dinosaur farts.

But let's suppose, for the sake of argument, that human activity *is* the problem, or at least a large part of the problem. Who's going to convince a billion or so Chinese and Indians hoping to leapfrog a millennium from the eleventh to the twenty-first century to grin and bear the grinding but green poverty of their lives? Between them, China and India are constructing four new coal-fired power plants per week.[7] Why are they turning to coal rather than to cleaner and more conscientious alternatives like solar energy? Because, for the moment, that's what works. Fossil fuels remain the economy-class ticket to modernity. Yeah, it might not be great for the ozone layer, but don't residents of China and India have a right to pursue, perhaps even to expect, the material comforts you and I take for granted? Like electricity and indoor plumbing? Like refrigerators and televisions and microwave ovens? Like personal computers and Internet access and, yes, down the road, even automobiles and bumper stickers?

Or should we just tell them to sign up for "therapy"?

"Global Warming Is Real. Deal with It."

Bumper sticker proposition: "Global warming is real." How should Americans deal with it? The United States currently creates 18 percent of the world's carbon emissions even though we're less than 5 percent of the world's population—one of the worst ratios on the planet.[8] (Then again, we're also the world's cop, the world's EMT, the world's philanthropist, the world's entertainer, the world's entrepreneur, the world's arbitrator, the world's scapegoat . . . and, yes, the world's moral conscience. The willingness to acknowledge such truths is, for the record, a measure of a liberal's intellectual seriousness.) So what should the United States do to lead the way to a greener tomorrow? What collective sacrifice is appropriate?

How about if we scrap our automobiles? According to a 2006 study by the nonprofit advocacy group Environmental Defense

Fund, U.S. cars and light trucks account for roughly half the greenhouse gases emitted by personal motor vehicles worldwide. The study notes that in 2004, the last year for which statistics were available, American automobiles belched out 314 million metric tons of CO_2—enough carbon to fill a freight train 50,000 miles long.[9] (You don't want to get caught at the cross signal as that thing rolls by.) Clearly, cars are a substantial part of our national carbon footprint. So why not just pull every car in the United States, with the possible exception of police and emergency vehicles, off the road? Make them into decorative planters, the more foliage the better, and provide every American access to public transportation?

Sure, it'll kill NASCAR, but I suspect a majority of liberals would be willing to put up with that . . .

But here's another idea. What if we get rid of our best friends?

According to a 2006 study by Robert and Brenda Vale, a husband-and-wife team of research fellows at Victoria University in New Zealand who specialize in sustainable living design, the carbon footprint of an average-size dog (including the land required to feed the farm animals consumed by Spot in his daily diet) is twice as large as the carbon footprint of a Toyota Land Cruiser (including construction, fuel and maintenance). The carbon footprint of the average cat is roughly equal to that of a Volkswagen Golf.[10] The Vales' estimates have since been confirmed by scientists at the Stockholm Environment Institute in York, England,[11] and the Earth Policy Institute in Washington, D.C.[12]

Consider: There are approximately seventy-five million domestic dogs in the United States. Their environmental impact thus equals approximately 150 million SUVs. Let's dwell on that number. *One hundred and fifty million SUVs.* As of 2006, there were about one hundred million SUVs on the road in the United States, out of a total of 250 million registered vehicles. So if we weaned ourselves off canine companionship, we'd achieve the same green goals as the elimination of every single SUV in America, plus another fifty million beyond that total.

That figure doesn't even include the ecoboon of ridding ourselves of cats. There are upwards of eighty-five million of them in the United States, each one snootier than the next, and each one equal, in terms of its environmental impact, to a Volkswagen Golf. Granted, the Golf is a significantly smaller SUV than the Land Cruiser, and the one-to-one Mr. Whiskers–Golf ratio means that the planetary advantage accrued by a blanket feline prohibition wouldn't generate the eye-popping numbers of its doggie counterpart. But a ban on all household pets—including not only dogs and cats but hamsters, gerbils, turtles, snakes, goldfish and (especially) bunny rabbits—would amount to, and perhaps even exceed, the ecodream of removing every motor vehicle from the roads of America. I'm not proposing killing the critters, mind you, just letting them expire and not replacing them . . .

People for the Ethical Treatment of Animals might have a hard time making the lifestyle adjustment. But, hey, like the bumper sticker says, "Global Warming Is Real. Deal with It."

My point isn't that we *should* ban dogs and cats. (Down, boy!) Rather, it's that liberals are always willing to sacrifice someone *else's* pursuit of happiness in their pursuit of green outcomes. If indeed human activity is responsible for global warming, we can *deal with it* in any number of ways. From the planet's perspective, ridding ourselves of domestic animals works as well as ridding ourselves of cars. The difference is that liberals like pets more than they like cars. So they'll turn up their noses at a guy in a

Hummer but bend over to caress a collie on a leash. Except here's the ugly truth: You can bike to and from the local campus to hear the latest sustainability lecture, bring reusable canvas bags to the local Whole Foods Market for your weekly shopping trip, but if you're going home to a couple of poodles, you might as well hang out a shingle that says *Earth Killer*.

"Faith-Based Government Burns People at the Stake"

The most famous sentence ever set to paper by an American did not emerge intact from a single pen. In his original draft of the Declaration of Independence, Thomas Jefferson wrote, "We hold these truths to be sacred and undeniable; that all men are created equal and independent, that from that equal creation they derive rights inherent and inalienable, among which are the preservation of life, and liberty, and the pursuit of happiness."

Benjamin Franklin and John Adams read that original draft and suggested minor alterations, which Jefferson incorporated into the final Declaration presented to the Second Continental Congress. The sentence became: "We hold these truths to be self-evident, that all men are created equal, that they are endowed by their Creator with certain unalienable Rights, that among these are Life, Liberty, and the pursuit of Happiness."

Though no one knows who made which edit, it's a safe bet that all three men gave that line a good going-over and agonized over its final form. Each change is thus worth noting. But let's focus on just two: (1) Why did "sacred and undeniable" become "self-evident"? and (2) what prompted the inclusion of the phrase "endowed by their Creator"?

The changes seem to pull in opposite directions, at least from the standpoint of separation-of-church-and-state liberals. You can imagine a colonial version of Bill Maher, dripping with trendy contempt for the Great Awakening, peering up from his opium-induced haze, shaking out the fleas from his powdered wig and nodding in approval at the switch from "sacred and undeniable" to "self-evident." *Get that superstitious tripe out of there!* But why would more thoughtful guys like Jefferson, Franklin and Adams prefer the latter to the former? Maybe because "sacred and undeniable" starts an argument, but "self-evident" ends one. If you say, "We hold these truths to be sacred and undeniable," you're laying the emphasis on the word *we*, telling the reader who you are: *We're the guys who believe these things.* On the other hand, if you say, "We hold these truths to be self-evident," you're stressing the reader's response, telling him, in effect, that if he doesn't agree, he's suffering from a mental deficiency; he can't muster a sufficient degree of rationality. Recall that the Declaration was written at the height of the Enlightenment—when congruence with human reason had begun to eclipse congruence with scripture as the ultimate gauge of truth. What is self-evident must be self-evident to all reasonable people. Those who fail to grasp what is self-evident, therefore, are being unreasonable. In 1776, that charge represents a significant intellectual smackdown.

The colonial Bill Maher might have nodded at the change from "sacred and undeniable" to "self-evident." But he would've gone batshit—in the colloquial of our current Maher—at the insertion of the phrase "endowed by their Creator." *Oh no, not Him again! Not the Imaginary Friend in the Sky!* So why did Jefferson, Franklin and Adams deem it necessary? We can rule out the idea that the mention of a "Creator" was meant as a straightforward signal of piety. Franklin and Jefferson were *deists*. That is, they believed in a Higher Power that governed the universe but not a personal God; indeed, Jefferson once literally cut up a New Testament, excising all the supernatural elements, in order to pare down the text to its moral core. Their Christianity—if it can even be called that—was watered down almost to the point of agnosticism. Adams was a more traditional believer, but his Unitarianism was among the least emotive of Christian denominations. So their collective decision to invoke a capital-*C* "Creator" as the source of men's equality must be taken as pragmatic, not devotional. But what does invoking a Creator accomplish?

Remember that Jefferson had originally written that "all men are created equal and independent," and "that from that equal creation they derive rights inherent and inalienable." The problem with that first version is that it's obviously false. Even if we grant that men are created independent—highly dubious in itself—they are certainly *not* created equal in any quantifiable way. Not physically. Not intellectually. Not even if we mean their hidden potentials. No matter how much I practice, I'll never be as good a basketball player as Michael Jordan. No matter how long I study, I'll never be as good a physicist as Albert Einstein. Judged by the characteristics they inherit from their biological parents—who, after all, are their lower-case-*c* creators—men are decidedly *unequal* in their creation. Therefore, their equality, if it does exist, must consist of an immeasurable quality, an intangible essence . . . or, in other words, a *soul*.

This is the signature recognition, the sine qua non, of natural law theory—which is the moral system through which Jefferson sought to make his case for American independence. On a collective level, the theory holds that the written-down laws of any government, including those of the king of England, must conform with, in Jefferson's words, the "Laws of Nature"—which may not be written down but which flow from "Nature's God" and which are thus binding on all people and governments. If the written-down laws stop conforming to the Laws of Nature, then the social contract is broken. The king no longer rules.

On an individual level, natural law holds that there is a Third Party, beyond a biological mother and father, involved in the act of human creation. Your two parents generated your material substance, the goop and soup of you; that much could be said of any mammal. But, according to natural law, God expresses His interest in every human being through the act of ensoulment—the creation of an individual soul—by virtue of which the human being becomes a person. And from that quality of personhood flow the inalienable rights of life, liberty and the pursuit of happiness. The genesis of this concept of personhood is, well, the book of Genesis. Specifically, Genesis 1:26–27: "So God created man in his own image, in the image of God created he him; male and female created he them." If the biblical passage makes sense, given the peculiarities to which human flesh is subject, the image of God in man must be the soul.

Natural law, in short, rests on the mystical singularity of the creation of mankind, on the notion that human beings are distinct from other creatures in that they alone are made in God's image and only in them can personhood inhere . . . and *persons* possess rights that every government must respect.

But in what sense is any of this "self-evident," as the Declaration, in its final form, insists? The phrase has the ring of mathematical certainty. But if you stop and think about it, the statement that all men are created equal is by no means "self-evident"—at

least not in the common sense of the term. Traditionally, a statement is self-evident only if it's true by definition. It is self-evident,
for example, that a triangle has fewer sides than a square. But
can we *really* say, with the same degree of certainty, that all men
are created equal? That they're endowed by their Creator with
inalienable rights? That those rights include life, liberty and the
pursuit of happiness?

Clearly, not.

As a matter of fact, the "self-evident" truth that all men are
created equal isn't even a rational statement. What U-Haul of em-
pirical data would ever suffice to prove or disprove it? It's not the
kind of statement you'd even bother to prove or disprove because
it's an article of faith. It only makes sense if you buy into the theol-
ogy of a soul-endowing God. There's no dancing around that. If
there's no such thing as a soul, then there's no way to make sense
of the entire passage. The rights to life, liberty and the pursuit of
happiness—that's just the bundled software.

You know where this analysis is going, don't you? It is sheer
nonsense to argue that America's historical separation of church
and state is absolute when the Declaration of Independence is
rooted in an article of faith. What is the Constitution, for that
matter, and the volumes and volumes of jurisprudence derived
from it, except the written-down laws designed to safeguard the
basic rights mentioned in the Declaration?

There is no "wall of separation between church and state"
in America. The metaphor is found nowhere in the Constitution—as many liberals wrongly believe. It comes from an 1802
letter by then-president Jefferson to the Baptists of Danbury, Con-
necticut. The Baptists had written Jefferson because they were

concerned that their state constitution had no explicit law guaranteeing them freedom to worship as they saw fit. Jefferson replied that they needn't worry since the First Amendment to the U.S. Constitution had built a "wall of separation between Church and State." Jefferson was right; the First Amendment rendered state guarantees of religious liberty redundant. But the wall metaphor itself was ill-conceived.[13] You can't build a wall between a house and its foundation. The foundation of the United States is the article of faith that all men are created equal and endowed by their Creator with basic rights. It's our creedal core.

Unfortunately, Jefferson's wall metaphor has taken on a life of its own. It has nested in the bosom of liberals. Many of them now imagine themselves manning the barricades of a besieged city, the last bastion of secular values, as wild-eyed, Bible-thumping hordes drive their battering rams against the outer wall, hoping to break through and start burning heretics. The slightest crack in the wall—a crèche outside the local post office, a sculpture of the Ten Commandments in a courthouse—and the hordes will surely break through, rush in and put an end to American civilization as we know it.

The trouble with that image is *the city itself is a church*. Not the kind of church you'd recognize on the side of the road, not the kind with a clergyman up front and a congregation praying in the pews, not the kind a sophomoric HBO comic would mock. But it's a church nevertheless, a church dedicated to the proposition that all men are created equal. If you miss that, you miss the point Lincoln was addressing at Gettysburg. You miss the long, winding, but inexorable road from "all men are created equal" to "all persons are created equal."

Jefferson's faith judgment became, over the course of two centuries, the magnetic north of the world's moral compass. It's the only reason the original city, that one up there on the hill, was ever worth dying for.

"Keep Your Laws off My Body"

January 22 has evolved into a national red-letter day of sorts, a day of ritual observance if not quite a holiday, to mark the anniversary of the Supreme Court's landmark 1973 *Roe v. Wade* decision. Commemorations abound, typically either guitar-strumming celebrations by pro-choice stalwarts or curbside prayer vigils by pro-life crusaders, and mainstream journals churn out perfunctory retrospectives. But four decades of back-and-forth advocacy have settled nothing. Abortion remains the most divisive issue in the United States since the abolition of slavery. In fact, the very details of the ruling seem to recede, year by year, deeper into a foam of overwrought rhetoric. Specifically, therefore: *Roe* guaranteed a woman's right to terminate a pregnancy in the first trimester (in all instances) and in the second trimester (to safeguard her own "well-being," broadly defined); only in the third trimester of pregnancy, the *Roe* decision held, could the rights of the fetus be taken into account and abortion restricted by the state.

Let's stipulate that there are serious philosophical and legal arguments on both sides of the abortion debate. "Keep your laws off my body" isn't one of them. Insisting that a woman has the right to terminate a pregnancy because she controls her own body is either demonstrably false or logically meaningless. Even if we grant the highly contentious point that the fetus is part of a woman's body, it is just not true that individual Americans, male or female, exercise *absolute* sovereignty over their own bodies. If that were the case, not only would forty-nine states have to join Nevada in legalizing prostitution, but every state would also have to permit the selling of internal organs for transplant and hiring out of wombs for gestation—which in turn would warrant the bodily exploitation of poor people by rich people. Not exactly a dream scenario for egalitarian-minded liberals. For good reason, therefore, there is no right to absolute sovereignty of the body. However, if we take the bodily sovereignty argument in a weaker sense—specifically, that a woman's right to control her own body includes the right to terminate a pregnancy—then what we're left with is a tautology: A woman should have the right to an abortion because a woman has the right to an abortion.

"Pro-Choice: No More Wire Hangers"

Almost as weak as the bodily sovereignty argument for upholding *Roe* is the pragmatic argument. Let's again grant the hidden premises, namely: (1) that if states were permitted to outlaw abortions altogether, many would likely do so; and (2) that women in those states who desired abortions but couldn't afford to travel would turn to "back alley" alternatives. This is, nevertheless, an attempt to resolve a moral question on strictly practical grounds. The danger is that identical logic could be applied, let's say, to dogfighting. Like abortion, dogfighting is likely to continue regardless of the sanctions against it. Legalization, therefore, would allow the government to regulate it and ensure its conduct under more wholesome conditions. (Michael Vick could run for national commissioner.) Of course, practical considerations can and do enter into our decisions about when to enforce a law; practical considerations can and do mitigate the penalties imposed when a law is broken. But practical considerations cannot in and of themselves determine the morality of a law.

Obviously, this isn't the right venue for a thorough analysis of the *Roe* decision.[14] But it's always useful to clear out a bit of the bumper sticker level of the debate.

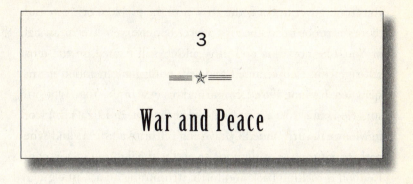

3

War and Peace

"Give Peace a Chance"

Let's admit the obvious up front: It's hard to argue with a dead Beatle. It's bad form, or at least it *feels* like bad form, given what we know of John Lennon's fate, to observe that the guy was never a deep thinker, that "Imagine," for all its haunting musical power, is as lyrically trite as a Hallmark card, and as morally windy as a fortune cookie. Poets, of course, don't have to worry about formulating policy; they don't even have to know what they're saying since the Muse is singing through them. That's the reason Plato never trusted them.

The thing about Lennon is that he sang like a poet but, by the late sixties, walked and talked like a prophet. Hell, he even looked the part: Hair down to his shoulders, beard down to his chest, dressed in billowing white fabrics. C'mon, you've seen the video a hundred times, whether you were born in 1946 or 1996, whether you think government is the answer to the problem or the reason there's a problem in the first place, because you live in an age of YouTube nostalgia and in a culture still fixated on the most self-righteous, self-centered and self-indulgent generation it ever spawned. It's June 1969. Lennon and his new bride, Yoko Ono, are sprawled out across a king-size bed at the Queen Elizabeth Hotel in Montreal, surrounded by fawning celebrity admirers and sympathetic journalists, calling for an end to the fighting in Vietnam. Lennon is rocking back and forth, strumming an acoustic guitar and singing: "All we are saying is give peace a chance."

How uncomplicated that sounded back in 1969! There were protest marches in downtown streets, student takeovers on college campuses, race riots in inner cities. Giving peace a chance struck me, at the time, as a damn fine suggestion. Of course, I was twelve years old back then . . .

It would take six more years, but Lennon would get his peace. The antiwar movement he helped inspire and came to epitomize wore down the will of the American public to sustain the military effort in Vietnam; the United States was forced to concede a costly, bitter battle in its decades-old proxy war against the Soviet Union—an enemy every bit as evil, every bit as genocidal, as Nazi Germany had been a generation before. America withdrew its troops from Vietnam, leaving South Vietnam at the mercy of the Soviet-sponsored communists to the north; in short order, the North Vietnamese army overran the south and united Vietnam under a single communist government.

Baby boom liberals had thus thwarted the American military, the greatest engine for individual liberty, collective prosperity and Enlightenment values the world has ever known. America's quitting the Southeast Asian battlefields had consequences beyond the borders of Vietnam. The same month Saigon fell to the communists of North Vietnam, the communist Khmer Rouge seized power in neighboring Cambodia. The Khmer Rouge then did what communists do: They began breaking eggs for their collectivization omelet. In pursuit of an agrarian utopia, they hunted down anyone with ties to the former government, anyone unfit for the physical rigors of farming, professionals and intellectuals (defined as anyone who wore glasses since that indicated literacy), ethnic and religious minorities . . . in other words, the usual suspects. By the time the Khmer Rouge government fell five years later, the killing fields were scattered with somewhere between 1,400,000 and 2,200,000 corpses . . . out of a total Cambodian population of only eight million.

America's decision to *give peace a chance* in Vietnam condemned not only that nation but its neighbor Cambodia to communist rule. The result was the worst per capita holocaust of the twentieth century. Yet the slogan still adorns liberals' car bumpers four decades later.

"End Terrorism: Reclaim Religion from Radical Fundamentalists"

Liberals, as a rule, value flexibility more than conservatives do. Yoga is a good example. Few things in life require more flexibility than yoga, which is why there's not much point in circulating a petition to safeguard the Second Amendment in a Bikram studio. Besides, liberals also like their Constitution flexible; they like the thought of it living and breathing, having its friends over for a cup of coffee, ordering Chinese takeout and changing with changing times . . . and if that means the Second Amendment no longer contains an individual right to bear arms, well, that's fine and dandy with them.

Liberals, as a rule, like their morality flexible as well. You know the old saying about how nature abhors a vacuum? The parallel in American politics is liberals abhor a judgment. *Who are we to judge other people,* they ask themselves, *when we haven't walked a mile in other people's moccasins?* Maybe, if we'd lived through their experiences, we would see things in another light. Isn't that what Einstein taught us with his theory of relativity?

Liberals especially like their religion flexible. They like the kind of religion that makes vague recommendations rather than spells out definite rules, the kind that says, "Well, you know, this might be one path to spiritual awakening, but of course there are many others, and hey that's a nice pair of moccasins you've got there, so would you mind if I tried them on?" This kind of religion flatters liberals, reassures them that regardless of the scummy things they're doing in their own lives, they're still nice people because their intentions are good and because God—if She exists—knows it.

That's the reason liberals dislike fundamentalism. It's not flexible. Religious fundamentalists believe in a hard-and-fast set of doctrines rooted in scripture, and they follow a strict moral code based on those doctrines, and fundamentalists will tell you, if you ask them, and often even if you don't ask them, that your soul is going straight to hell if you're not doing the things they do.

That's just the sort of talk that gets under liberals' skin. They think it's crazy. Worse than crazy. They think it's *judgmental.* Nothing irks a liberal more than the thought that he's being judged, except maybe the thought that he's being judged by God.

The fact that fundamentalism irks liberals also colors their attitude toward America's ongoing war with totalitarian Islam. There's no need to take sides, which would entail a moral judgment. Instead, liberals can blame the entire conflict on dueling fundamentalisms. It's the religious crackpots on both sides, clinging to literal interpretations of ancient crackpot scriptures, who egg on the rest of us to make war. If reasonable people could tune out the fundamentalists in their midst, the argument goes, both sides would at last come to their senses. The fighting would stop.

You can see the immediate attraction of such thinking for liberals. It means the good guys–bad guys model doesn't apply. The true villains don't inhabit the battlefield; they lurk behind the scene, pulling strings and shaping policies, duping others to do their dirty work in the name of a God who might or might not exist but who surely has nothing to do with the bigoted, irrational texts the fundamentalists revere. You need look no further than the texts themselves—the Bible and the Koran—to witness the dangers of literalism.

There's even a veneer of plausibility in such an account . . . provided that your grasp of religious history runs no deeper than the sophomoric clichés expressed on an average Bill Maher panel discussion.[1] Liberals love to trot out Leviticus 20:13—"If a man lies with a male as with a woman, both of them have committed an abomination; they shall be put to death"—as proof that Judeo-Christian scriptures are no less vicious and hateful, and no less capable of inspiring mayhem, than their Islamic counterparts.

In reality, however, the Leviticus passage proves the exact reverse of what liberals want it to prove . . . that is, that the true villain in the current struggle between the Judeo-Christian West

and the Islamic East is fundamentalism on both sides. The Old
Testament explicitly commands believers to kill men who engage
in homosexual intercourse. Yet no rabbi or pastor with any sort
of following will stand up in front of his congregation and call
for death to gay men. He may cite the words of Leviticus as a
reason to oppose legalizing same-sex marriage; he may cite them
to argue against openly gay men leading scout troops or marching in ethnic pride parades. But no matter how committed he is
to fundamentalist principles, he's not going to demand that gay
men be rounded up and murdered. Fatal literalism, within the
Judeo-Christian tradition, is now off the table.

By contrast, fatal literalism is alive and well among Muslim
fundamentalists. The Koran, for instance, instructs women to
cover their heads for the sake of modesty (sura 33:59). This seems
at first glance no more burdensome than the requirement, say,
that Jewish men wear yarmulkes. But in March 2002, fourteen
young girls perished during a fire at a middle school in Mecca
when the city's religious police—also known as the Committee for the Propagation of Virtue and the Prevention of Vice—
wouldn't allow firefighters to rescue them from the burning
building. Why? Because the girls weren't wearing proper head
coverings, and thus couldn't be seen in public.

As much as liberals want to equate Islamic fundamentalism
with Jewish or Christian fundamentalism, they're comparing
apples and oranges. Or, if you prefer, fundamentalism-old-school
and fundamentalism-lite. It's true that the words of the Bible are
as handy (or *almost* as handy) for justifying homicidal, even genocidal, acts as those of the Koran. But Jews and Christians have
gotten past doing it. Muslims haven't. Evidence can be found in

the monthly fatwas issued by influential Muslim clerics, calling for death and destruction to be visited upon infidels—a category broad enough to encompass anyone doing anything the clerics happen to dislike.

The question is, how did we, and how did they, get here?

The short answer is that Islam took a wrong turn at the Enlightenment. If you like your truth straight up, with no special pleading or apologizing, there it is. The Muslim world never absorbed the moderating spirit of rational inquiry and religious tolerance that allowed the Christian nation states of Europe and America to flourish; that's the main reason the West left Islam in the dust, literally and figuratively, a quarter of a millennium ago. Until then, Islam and Christianity were careening side by side down the same hellish highway, exchanging bloody crusades, enslaving conquered and helpless peoples, burning and mutilating nonbelievers. Then came the exit marked *Enlightenment*. Christianity got off . . . and got on the twisting, bumpy road to the modern world.

Islam missed the turn altogether.

Thus began that religion's long, dreary slide into civilization's Dumpster, the current residence of more than a billion Muslims. What is the state of Islam, *now*? It's four centuries and counting of degenerate theocracies, military dictatorships and cultural wastelands in which the only reliably inspiring question has become "Who did this to us?"

If liberals want to blame the ongoing war on terror on the pre-Enlightenment Islamic fundamentalism, they won't be far from the truth. But the notion that fundamentalism per se is the problem is absurd, untenable. Jewish and Christian fundamentalisms are red herrings. Their only purpose in the discussion is to distract liberals from the cognitive necessity of discerning the good guys from the bad guys in the war on terror.

"Coexist" (with iconic symbols of Judaism, Christianity and Islam)

Toward the end of the musical *My Fair Lady*, Henry Higgins, the erudite but consistently oblivious British speech professor, suddenly discovers that Eliza Doolittle, the impoverished flower girl he's attempted to transform into a refined English lady, has feelings of her own—she's not just a lump of clay to be molded into whatever shape he wants. He is baffled by her sudden flood of emotions and launches into a comic tune called "A Hymn to Him." The lyrics address a fundamental question: "Why can't a woman be more like a man?" Higgins is genuinely dismayed that women aren't just feminine copies of men; they're not "regular chaps" willing to "help you through any mishaps." Even their thought processes are alien; they don't reason things out soberly and logically. They always seem concerned with "straightening up their hair" . . . but overlook "the mess that's inside."

The song is played for laughs. The audience realizes that it tells you next to nothing about the actual mental lives of men and women, but it tells you everything you need to know about the arrogance and bigotry of Henry Higgins.

There's a similar arrogance and bigotry at work among liberals who ride around with a bumper sticker like "Coexist"—as if a clever graphic merging of iconic symbols proves that religious differences are ultimately insignificant, that spiritual agendas can be reconciled.

You can understand the sentiment, at least on a certain level. When it comes to the ongoing war against totalitarian Islam, liberals want to remain above the fray. They see no necessity in the conflict, or in any conflict, and thus want to avoid taking sides. If only *all* people learned to understand and respect one another, the situation would work itself out. Coexistence, after all, requires tolerance, and the word *tolerance*, conveniently enough, can also be purchased in icon-mingling bumper sticker form.

Except that imagining a world of peaceful coexistence, or urging universal tolerance among diverse people, is *not* adopting a neutral position in the ongoing war. Rather, it amounts to taking the side of the post-Enlightenment West against pre-Enlightenment Islam. As much as liberals want to stay on the sidelines, they're right in the thick of it. Their prayers for peace—a peace in which individuals are free to act according to the dictates of their conscience—place them squarely on the side of cultural heterogeneity over unity of belief, of personal autonomy over selfless obedience, of reason over faith. Ride around with a "Coexist" bumper sticker in downtown Islamabad and you're liable to get your head handed to you.

Literally.

Henry Higgins could not wrap his mind around the fact that Eliza Doolittle arrived at his doorstep with a full set of human thoughts and feelings, that she was more than the sum of his effects on her. Likewise, liberals cannot wrap their minds around the fact that Muslim radicals are thinking, feeling human beings; their inner lives are not determined merely, or even primarily, by their attitudes toward us. On the contrary, the psychic justifications for Islamic terrorism can be found in an intellectually accessible and, in its own way, profoundly moving philosophy that stands in direct opposition to the liberal democratic institutions of the West.

The key figure, according to a consensus of scholars in Islamic studies, is the Egyptian fundamentalist thinker Sayyid Qutb (1906–66), whose writings form the basis for radical Islam's struggle against Western ascendancy. Qutb's signature contribution to Muslim thought was to update the concept of *jahiliyya*. For centuries, *jahiliyya* had signified the state of ignorance in the world prior to the advent of Islam; according to Qutb, however, *jahiliyya* should also be understood as the underlying spirit of decadence and corruption that exists in all times and all places—and which Muslims are duty-bound to fight against. There can be no middle ground. "Islam cannot accept any compromise with *jahiliyya*," Qutb wrote. "Either Islam will remain or *jahiliyya*. . . . The mixing and co-existence of truth and falsehood is impossible. Command belongs to Allah or else to *jahiliyya*."[2] What was required, for Muslims, was to live under the strict Islamic code of laws called the sharia. It was the only way to ensure that they were living the way Allah intended.

Despite the sharia's rigidity, Qutb argued that it was the sole source of true liberation since the sharia came straight from God. Either human beings were ruled by God or they were ruled by other human beings; there was no distinction, on this level, between an absolute dictatorship or a representative democracy. Both amounted to the rule of men over men—which, according to Qutb, was always a form of oppression. (It's worth noting that Qutb reserved many of his most virulent criticisms for secular-minded Muslims.) Only the rule of God provided people with freedom. Thus Qutb rejected out of hand the entire Enlightenment project, which sought to separate church from state.

Whatever else might be said about Qutb's worldview, it represents a straightforward, coherent, easily understood system of beliefs—a system that has been vastly influential among Islamic radicals, including Osama bin Laden.[3] Jihad is legitimized, in the radicals' eyes, as the struggle against *jahiliyya*. The only question is how far jihad is aimed. The short-term goal would consist of casting out the infidel Jews and Christians from Islamic holy lands and recapturing the holy cities of Mecca and Medina from the *jahiliyya*-tainted Saudi regime; the long-term goal would consist of subjugating the non-Islamic West, which means defeating the United States, in order, first, to keep its corrupting influences out of Islam, and, ultimately, to liberate the West itself from the suffocating darkness of Enlightenment secularism.

It is a *totalitarian* movement in the truest sense.

The war against totalitarian Islam, on a fundamental level, is therefore a struggle between Enlightenment and anti-Enlightenment forces. To overlook this first truth is to misapprehend the nature of the conflict. To be sure, there are other elements involved. Ethnic rivalries. Nationalist movements. Regional and tribal loyalties. Religious schisms. Historical grievances. Natural resources. Global economics. The war is a witches' brew of divided allegiances and score-settling. But at its bottom, beneath the claims and counterclaims, the war is between two irreconcilable visions for the future of mankind. The forces of Enlightenment, committed to rational inquiry and religious tolerance, manifest in liberal democratic rule, versus the forces of anti-Enlightenment, committed to faithful obedience to a divine will, manifest in sharia rule.

It is Thomas Jefferson versus Sayyid Qutb.

Liberals do not accept this analysis. They *cannot* accept this analysis because it means that Muslim radicals are morally accountable, that *we* didn't make them who and what they are. They didn't arrive at our doorstep as a list of accusations against the West. They arrived as human beings with a cultural heritage and a belief system that cannot *coexist* with ours, that cannot *tolerate* who we are and what we do.

Because, to be blunt about it, we're up in their faces. Muslim radicals realize the stakes involved. Liberals do not. Liberals join hands at antiwar rallies to sing, "Why can't a jihadi be more like a Quaker?" Hmmm, let's see. Could it be that we're stealing the hearts and minds of their children? On television, radio and the Internet, in glossy magazines, newspapers and paperbacks, on movie screens, home videos and CDs, Americans are absolutely everywhere, acting out in every conceivable way to seduce the next generation of Muslims away from the path of righteousness. We are bombarding them with the flotsam and jetsam of our pop media, from Eminem's potty mouth to Britney Spears's gyrating pelvis, from the Rock's arched eyebrow to Serena Williams's tennis skirts, from the brawling on *The Jerry Springer Show* to the mincing on *Project Runway*. Such ephemera are endured by us, the lowbrow excretions of our dedication to highbrow ideals like personal autonomy, artistic expression and free enterprise. For radical Islam, they are the toxic images of a steady spiritual genocide being wrought upon them.

You know what? It's pissing them off. Don't take my word for it. Here's an excerpt from Osama bin Laden's 2002 letter to America, which is worth quoting a length:

We call upon you to be a people of manners, principles, honor and purity; to reject the immoral acts of fornication, homosexuality, intoxicants, gambling and trading with interest. . . . You are the nation who, rather than being ruled by the Sharia of Allah in its Constitution and Laws, choose to invent your own laws as you will and desire. You separate religion from your policies, contradicting the pure nature which affirms Absolute Authority to the Lord and your Creator. . . . You are a nation that permits Usury, which has been forbidden by all the religions. As a result of this, in all its different forms and guises, the Jews have taken control of your economy . . . making you their servants and achieving their aims at your expense. . . . You are a nation that permits the production, trading and usage of intoxicants and drugs. . . . You are a nation that permits acts of immorality, and you consider them to be pillars of person freedom. . . . You are a nation that permits gambling in all its forms. . . . You are a nation that exploits women like consumer products or advertising tools calling upon customers to purchase them. . . . You are a nation that practices the trade of sex in all its forms, directly and indirectly. Giant corporations are established on this, under the name of art, entertainment, tourism and freedom. . . . And because of all this, you have been described in history as a nation that spreads diseases that were unknown to man in the past. Go ahead and boast to the nations of man that you brought them AIDS as a Satanic American invention.

So there you have it. Straight from the source. If American foreign policy is the root cause of terrorism, why would Osama bother to comment on our domestic culture?[4] Was he just looking for an op-ed gig at the *New York Times?* You either take the radicals at their word or you don't. Liberals don't. They prefer to see Muslims as moral clay, misshapen only because of the geo-political wrongs—real and imagined—done to them by the West, waiting to be reshaped in our image once their grievances have been addressed.

It ain't gonna happen.

The war in which America is now engaged is a death struggle between, on the one hand, traditional Islamic values of pious sub-mission and spiritual purity, and, on the other hand, ingrained Enlightenment values of rational inquiry and religious tolerance. The two sides cannot *coexist.* Either we have to stop being us, or they have to stop being them. There's no sidestepping that point. If you haven't figured it out, and the vast majority of liberals still haven't, then the past decade of American foreign policy makes no sense except in sinister conspiratorial terms.

Hey, maybe it *is* really all about oil, or about Zionism, or about George W. Bush's Oedipal Complex. . . .

"No, Really, Why Did We Invade Iraq?"

On May 1, 2010, my friend Linda and I were walking through Times Square on our way back to our midtown Manhattan apart-ments from an early dinner in Greenwich Village. The going, as usual, was slow. It was a Saturday night, around six-thirty, and Broadway, between Forty-Second and Forty-Eighth Streets, was jammed. There were theatergoers hustling to dinner reservations in order to make their eight o'clock showtimes; tourists standing and pointing at the rhythmic wash of neon lights; cabbies honk-ing at one another and at food delivery guys on bicycles, who were pretending not to hear them; struggling actors dressed up as Disney and Sesame Street characters, charging a buck to pose with children; young comedians urging passersby to check out the evening's lineup at Carolines; street peddlers hawking faux designer purses, scarves and perfumes; a row of Asian sketch artists trying to flag down potential customers; a troupe of break-dancers somersaulting and spinning on their heads for cash contributions; a young black guy banging on a drum kit made out of paint buckets; an old black guy with a miniature generator playing electric guitar; and another old black guy playing a saxophone.

It took perhaps ten minutes, but Linda and I fought our way through the crowd and arrived at our apartments without incident.

The following morning we discovered that we'd passed within thirty feet of a large car bomb at Broadway and Forty-Fifth Street at the exact time it was supposed to detonate. That bomb had been planted by a thirty-year-old naturalized U.S. citizen from Pakistan whom the press would dub the Times Square Bomber. His device sparked and smoked for several minutes but failed to explode. It was noticed by a T-shirt vendor, who alerted a cop. The cop called for backup, which included the police bomb squad. Using remote-controlled robots, the bomb squad broke the car's windows and discovered three gas-grill-size tanks of propane, two five-gallon cans of gasoline, a large locker filled with fertilizer, an assortment of fireworks intended to ignite the propane and gas, and two alarm clocks used as timers.[5] The device was extinguished with no injuries to first responders or civilians.

The takeaway, however, is this: If not for the technical incompetence of a Muslim dirtbag named Faisal Shahzad, Linda and I would likely be dead. So, too, would hundreds of other civilians—a literal cross section of humanity, including mothers with their babies in strollers, wide-eyed teenagers in tour groups, and husbands and wives out for a night on the town. They would be dead because Islam justifies, or at least is understood by millions of believers to justify, setting off a bomb in Times Square. Note the phrase "Muslim dirtbag." Neither term by itself accounts for the terrorist act he attempted to perpetrate; both terms, however, are equally complicit in it. It might have been a crapshoot of nature and nurture that wrought a specimen like Shahzad, but it was Islam that inspired him, that gave his fecal stain of a life its depth and its justification. He understands what liberals do not: "War on Terror" is nothing more than a euphemism for the War Against Totalitarian Islam. Toppling the Taliban in Afghanistan, crushing Saddam in Iraq and putting the screws to the mullahs in Iran is one and the same war. It's the war Shahzad is fighting. If we decided tomorrow to walk away from it, it would find us again in short order.

New York mayor Michael Bloomberg characterized Shahzad's bomb as "amateurish,"[6] a point underscored by the use of fireworks and alarm clocks. Shahzad thus joins the ranks of a rapidly growing clown posse of terrorists whose plans have gone awry. There's Richard Reid, the Afghani-trained "Shoe Bomber," who in 2001 attempted to take down a passenger plane by setting a match to explosives concealed in one of his shoes; he was subdued by fellow passengers but not before partially fulfilling his jihad by biting the thumb of a female flight attendant. Reid, in turn, provided the inspiration for Umar Farouk Abdulmutallab, the Yemen-trained "Underwear Bomber," who in 2009 attempted to take down a passenger plane with explosives concealed in his drawers. He, too, failed but sustained second-degree burns to his hands, thighs and genitals.

Who could forget the Dukas of Jersey? Three Muslim brothers whose kinfolk entered the United States illegally through Mexico when they were children, they were notable only for a rash of petty crime and bad driving—among them, they'd accumulated about fifty traffic citations—before joining with three coreligionists in a plot to stage a guerrilla attack on the army base in Fort Dix. They practiced for the assault throughout 2005, videotaping themselves in the woods firing semiautomatic weapons and shouting, "Allahu Akbar!" But then, in early 2006, they made a minor tactical error. They went to a local Circuit City to convert their videotape to DVD. One of the store's employees noticed the contents of the tape and called the police. A full-scale investigation was launched, and the group was rolled up without getting off a shot at their intended target.[7] Even more ill-conceived was a 2007 plot by three Muslim men to blow up fuel tanks and a forty-mile pipeline in and around Kennedy Airport in New York City—a physical impossibility given the fail-safes built into the system. Their ringleader, Russell Defreitas, a native of Guyana and naturalized U.S. citizen, was interested not only in the body count but in the lasting damage to the American psyche: "Anytime you hit Kennedy, it is the most hurtful thing to do to the United States . . . they love JFK, he's like *the man*. If you hit that . . . it's like you can kill the man twice."[8] Defreitas followed in the great cerebral tradition of Kashmir-born Iyman Faris, also a naturalized American citizen, who thought he could take down the Brooklyn Bridge with a blowtorch. He confessed to the plot in 2003.[9]

Perhaps the finest recent example of jihadist masterminds at work came in June 2007 with a plot to explode twin car bombs in the heart of London. Conceived and executed by a cell of Muslim physicians and PhDs who crammed the cars with gasoline canisters and nails, the devices were discovered when passersby smelled gas fumes. They were quickly defused by British bomb squads on June 29. The following day, however, Kafeel Ahmed, a twenty-eight-year-old Indian Muslim with a doctorate in engineering who had rigged the bombs, took a more direct approach and drove a Jeep Cherokee packed with gasoline and explosives into the passenger terminal at Glasgow International Airport in Scotland. The only victim turned out to be Ahmed—who sustained burns to more than 90 percent of his body and died a month later.

Despite the educational backgrounds of the conspirators, the plot was striking for its slapstick ineptitude. Plastic syringes used as firing mechanisms in the first two cars didn't spark; the mobile phones that were supposed to ignite the syringes rang and rang as the terrorists tried repeatedly to detonate the bombs from remote locations. This made the conspiracy exceptionally easy to crack using call records. And when Ahmed rammed his Jeep into the Glasgow terminal the next day, the car at first failed to explode. Witnesses came to his aid, thinking that the crash was an accident, until he climbed out of the wreck and started pouring out the gas canisters . . . which in turn ignited the engine and engulfed him in flames.[10]

Such incidents are, in a paradoxical way, both unnerving and soothing. They remind us of the severe degree of difficulty built into successful terrorist operations in the West, such as the March 11, 2004, train bombings in Madrid, the July 7, 2005, subway and bus bombings in London and, above all, the September 11, 2001, commercial airliner attacks in the United States. Far more frequent are the foiled plots, the Wile E. Coyote martyrs who self-destruct before they can do damage.

Realistically, however, we shouldn't take too much comfort in the failure rate among jihadists in Europe and America. Because, for the moment at least, the first-stringers are still tied up in Iraq and Afghanistan. That's what President Bush meant when he insisted, again and again, that we were fighting the terrorists "over there" so that we didn't have to fight them here—though liberals cannot seem to wrap their minds around this elementary point. There's no home field advantage in postmodern warfare. Whenever geopolitics allows, you want to go after terrorists where they live. Whatever minor edge the terrorists gain from fighting in their own backyard is more than offset by the fact that it's their stuff getting broken and their friends and relatives getting killed.

Terrorists, of course, would much rather fight us here. But staging an attack like 9/11 necessitates recruiting, preparing and supplying operatives who are skilled enough to carry out the mission yet rabid enough never to question the morality of what they're doing. That combination of blinkered competence and disregard for human life is found from time to time in New York City cabdrivers. Otherwise it is exceedingly rare. Suicide savants don't grow on trees. Tracking them down and training them up requires large sums of cash.

Money, in the final analysis, is the ultimate weapon of mass destruction. (It's the one WMD Saddam had indisputably stockpiled prior to the American invasion in 2003.) Self-starters, even well-heeled ones like the guys who botched the London and Glasgow jobs, cannot, as a rule, shell out the necessary funds and overcome the technological hurdles to pull off a major attack. For that, you need the kind of operating budgets that usually come from global organizations like Al Qaeda or from sovereign governments like Iran. But Al Qaeda and Iran, in case you haven't noticed, are currently too preoccupied with what's going on in their own neck of the woods to divert much of their terrorism resources elsewhere. That equation will change, without question, if it turns out that America has wound down the conflicts in Iraq and Afghanistan prematurely.

Without the worry of nascent democracies in their backyards, Al Qaeda and Iran will be free to start fielding their varsity teams over here.

The liberal belief that the blood and treasure spent on the war in Iraq was wasted is, of course, unshakable. It's settled doctrine. No Iraqi outcome, including the emergence of a stable liberal democracy, will convince liberals that the costs were worth it. Part of the reason is Bush Derangement Syndrome (about which, more later). But the Bush administration itself must also be faulted because it rested so much of the case for invading Iraq on Saddam's weapons of mass destruction—which he turned out not to possess. That strategic blunder has, in effect, licensed liberals to disregard the possibility of a better future for the Iraqi people and harp in perpetuity on the failure to find WMDs.

But what if the worst-case scenario transpires? What if the American military withdraws, and Iraq soon thereafter descends into widespread ethnic and sectarian violence, with Iran backing the Shiites, and Saudi Arabia backing the Sunnis, and the Kurds looking out for their own interests? Are the Iraqi people worse off than they were under the tyranny of the wretched Hussein clan? It's a debatable point. You can argue that even in that worst-case scenario, even amid the chaos of multiple civil wars, the people would still have a fighting chance to arrive at a decent civil society. Stranger things have happened.

To be clear, though, whenever liberals insist that the war in Iraq was a waste of American resources, they're saying, whether they choose to admit it or not, that Saddam should still be in power. There's no weaseling out of that either/or. His regime wasn't teetering. He wasn't boxed in by United Nations sanctions—though the sanctions were exacting a horrific toll on the Iraqi people, a toll that far exceeded the body count of the postinvasion insurgency (again, specifics to come). If you say that America should've stayed out of Iraq, you're saying that the Iraqi status quo of February 2003 was preferable to the human and financial costs of America's intervention. It's not an untenable position. But you can't argue it and dance around the question of Saddam. Given the chance to unmake history, you'd keep Saddam in place and keep the troops home.

Fire up the wood chipper, and march out the dissidents . . .

What's indisputable, in the final analysis, is that in the decade that followed 9/11, the United States escaped another large-scale attack—an attack that almost every security expert and defense strategist assured us was inevitable. As grizzled jihadists flocked to the battlefields of Afghanistan and Iraq to face off against the American military, and more often than not get introduced to their seventy-two virgins, we on the home front confronted sorry sacks of shit like Russell Defreitas, Umar Farouk Abdulmutallab and Faisal Shahzad.

If it accomplished nothing else, the war in Iraq bought us time. It bought us a full decade to harden targets and isolate nut jobs, to refine watch lists and infiltrate mosques.

When the varsity team shows up next time, we'll be expecting them.

4

Hero Worship

"Free Mumia"

Mumia Abu-Jamal became an honorary citizen of Paris in 2003. Three years later, a street was named after him in the city's suburb of Saint-Denis. He wasn't able to attend either ceremony, however, because he was serving a life sentence for the murder of a Philadelphia police officer.

It's a sentence Abu-Jamal earned. On December 9, 1981, Danny Faulkner, a twenty-five-year-old cop, pulled over a car driven by William Cook—Abu-Jamal's younger brother—for a traffic violation. When Faulkner tried to handcuff him, Cook resisted, and as the two of them struggled, Abu-Jamal, driving a taxi in the neighborhood, spotted them, jumped from his cab and shot Faulkner in the back. Cook fled the scene as Faulkner collapsed to the ground. But Faulkner managed to wheel around and shoot Abu-Jamal in the chest. Abu-Jamal recoiled, then crawled back over to Faulkner and pumped four more shots into him, including one between his eyes, killing him.

Mumia Abu-Jamal is a cop killer. Full stop. The police found him holding the murder weapon, which was registered in his name, and slumped beside the body of Danny Faulkner. Ballistics tests proved that the .38-caliber bullets that killed Faulkner had been fired from Abu-Jamal's gun. During his 1982 trial, a female security guard at the hospital where he'd been taken to treat his injuries testified that she heard Abu-Jamal say, "I shot the mother-fucker, and I hope the motherfucker dies."

Next to Abu-Jamal, O. J. Simpson looks like Alfred Dreyfus.

Nevertheless, absurd conspiracy theories have circulated for decades about Abu-Jamal's innocence. His supporters—including such liberal luminaries as activists Angela Davis, Ramsey Clark and Noam Chomsky; actors Susan Sarandon, Alec Baldwin and Mike Farrell; authors Alice Walker, Maya Angelou and E. L. Doctorow; directors Spike Lee and Oliver Stone; rappers Chuck D and Mos Def; and rockers Rage Against the Machine and the Beastie Boys—seduced by Abu-Jamal's Rasta-next-door good looks and Idiot's Guide grasp of Marxism, insist that the police framed him. Why? Because, when he wasn't out driving taxis or killing cops, Abu-Jamal was a member of the Black Panthers and a two-bit journalist. Thus, their theories go, he had to be silenced.

Abu-Jamal has long insisted that he's a political prisoner, apparently having convinced himself that he wasn't really a high school dropout who'd been fired from his part-time radio gig and forced to drive a cab at night but rather a bona fide revolutionary, a threat to the socioeconomic establishment, jailed not for a brutal murder but for speaking the truth to power: "Capital's voice (the media) and their agents (the politicians) unite in a chorus of support for their legalized killers, who bomb babies with impunity . . . who shoot unarmed kids in their cars, and unarmed African emigrants, whose only capital crime is being Black in modern-day America."

Like many jailbirds before him, in other words, Abu-Jamal has lost touch with his own insignificance. He's less a man at this point than a series of poses. He envisions himself locked in a life-and-death battle against the government of the United States and has learned to regurgitate agitprop the way a trained rat learns to hit a lever in its cage for a crumb of cheese. But in Abu-Jamal's case, the cage *is* the cheese. His ongoing incarceration, as well as the celebrity cause it has inspired, is evidence that he matters.

The fact that French elites would succumb to Abu-Jamal's rodent charm should not surprise us. Paris, after all, was where the Swiss-born philosopher Jean-Jacques Rousseau set up permanent shop in the eighteenth century—and therein lies a larger point about contemporary liberals' habit of romanticizing criminality. It was Rousseau who argued that human beings are corrupted by modern society, that their natural moral impulses and egalitarian feelings are degraded by the social institutions that rule their lives—institutions that inspire competition and greed rather than cooperation and compassion.

If society itself is the cause of human evil, then antisocial behavior acquires a halo of righteousness. The rebel is redeemed not by his cause but by the mere fact of his rebellion. Indeed, we'd all be rebels if our spirits were pure enough, and if our consciences hadn't been co-opted by the powers that be.

The cultural influence of Rousseau's philosophy, especially on the political left, is hard to overstate. Within a generation, the English poet William Blake was so drunk on the notion of rebellion for its own sake that he viewed Satan ("Better to reign in hell than serve in heaven") rather than Jesus as the true hero of John Milton's epic poem *Paradise Lost*—an interpretation that would have spun Milton in his grave like a Duncan top.

The conceptual leap from celebrating the rebel to celebrating the criminal is not far. Every criminal act is like a miniature rebellion—even though the criminal himself may not think of it as such. The criminal, indeed, can be romanticized as the canary in the moral coal mine, a soul so affronted by the evil status quo that he's left with no choice but to break the law. The French writer and serial lawbreaker Jean Genet (1910–86) was thus immortalized as "St. Genet"—seized by "the vertigo of those beyond repair"—by the Marxist philosopher Jean-Paul Sartre. It's worth noting that Genet himself was drawn, later in life, to violent criminality dressed up as rebellion, palling around with Yasser Arafat and the Palestine Liberation Organization, and Huey Newton and the Black Panthers.

The Panthers—who began their existence as the Ku Klux Klan in snazzier outfits before branching out into drug dealing, prostitution and murder for hire—have long enjoyed a devoted following among well-heeled liberals. The composer-conductor Leonard Bernstein (1918–90) harbored a full-fledged man-crush on several Panther leaders, once hosting a fund-raising party for the group, attended by scores of Manhattan socialites . . . an event satirized by Tom Wolfe in his 1970 essay "Radical Chic: That Party at Lenny's."

If any one figure embodies liberals' adolescent fascination with criminal behavior it is Norman Mailer. In his famous 1957 essay "The White Negro," Mailer offers us the following meditation on the hypothetical murder of a shopkeeper by two young men:

It can of course be suggested that it takes little courage for two strong eighteen-year-old hoodlums, let us say, to beat in the brains of a candy-store keeper. . . . Still, courage of a sort is necessary, for one murders not only a weak fifty-year-old man but an institution as well, one violates private property, one enters into a new relation with the police and introduces a dangerous element into one's life. The hoodlum is therefore daring the unknown, and so no matter how brutal the act, it is not altogether cowardly.[1]

Whether the shopkeeper Mailer imagines is white, and the hoodlums black—as has often been assumed, given the title of the essay—is irrelevant. What matters is Mailer's analysis of the act. Crime is never meaningless or petty; it is always an expression of an existential struggle. To commit a crime is to *commit*. It is authentic, natural, brave. The criminal is *transgressing* the law rather than merely breaking it. The murder of the shopkeeper is, in the final analysis, a cry of freedom.

Mailer put his theory into practice in 1977, twenty years after the publication of "The White Negro." He took up the cause of Jack Henry Abbott, a lifelong convict whose rap sheet included forgery, bank robbery and murder. Abbott had written Mailer a fan letter from prison; in the exchange of letters that followed, Abbott offered Mailer insights about the brutalities of life behind bars. Mailer, in turn, collected Abbott's letters and got them published under the title *In the Belly of the Beast*. When Abbott came up for parole in June 1981, Mailer campaigned publicly and passionately on his behalf. Prison officials—who knew Abbott much better than Mailer did—had deep misgivings. But Mailer's celebrity carried the day, and Abbott was released.

Six weeks after his release, Abbott wandered into a Manhattan café wanting to use the toilet. Richard Adan, a twenty-two-year-old waiter and aspiring actor, told him the restrooms were for customers only . . . at which point Abbott pulled out a knife and stabbed Adan to death. Abbott fled the scene but was arrested several weeks later in Louisiana. Incredibly, at his trial for manslaughter in January 1982, Abbott still attracted celebrity admirers. Besides Mailer, the author Jerzy Kosinski and actors Christopher Walken and Susan Sarandon voiced their support for Abbott. Sarandon, who'd later speak out on behalf of Mumia Abu-Jamal, was pregnant during Abbott's trial. She eventually named her baby "Jack Henry" in his honor.

This time, however, the glitz and glamour didn't rescue Abbott. He was convicted of manslaughter and sentenced to fifteen years to life. He died in prison in 2002.

"Che Guevara: Until Victory Always"

When asked why his epic 2008 biopic on Ernesto Che Guevara needed to run a whopping four hours, coproducer and star Benicio del Toro squinted into the cameras and replied, "That is a question for Che. Why such a fulfilled life? We believe that this is the shortest film about Che Guevara's revolutionary life that could be made."

Well, no.

The shortest film about Che's revolutionary life that could be made actually *was* made in the 1980s. It ran thirty seconds. In it, a couple of scruffy, paramilitary-looking, motorcycle-riding cartoon cockroaches decide to "take over" a kitchen, running amok until a giant muscle-bound can of Raid appears and "kills them dead."

Guevara, in reality, belongs to that species of human vermin who attach themselves to a charismatic villain—in Che's case, Fidel Castro; in Heinrich Himmler's case, Adolf Hitler; in Khalid Sheikh Mohammed's case, Osama bin Laden—and enact their murderous agendas until the countervailing forces of history rise up and end their pathetic careers. Granted, Che is more photogenic than either the lipless stick figure Himmler or the hairy-backed Super Mario Brother KSM. It's hard to imagine either of them ever moving a gross of T-shirts the way Che does. But the fact that his brand continues to sell is a testament to the grotesque historical ignorance of liberals, who buy up Che merchandise the way Disneyland visitors buy up mouse ears.

Indeed, one of the ongoing mysteries of American popular culture is why communism is sold more often and more effectively than Nazism or Islamism. Why are young communists viewed as idealistic and kind of cute whereas young Nazis and young Islamists are viewed as hateful and distinctly creepy? If you're going to raise a glass to the heroic workers on May Day, why not to the storm troopers on the anniversary of Kristallnacht? Why not to Al Qaeda on September 11? Can it be just a matter of public relations? Why does an obsessive Nazi-hunter like Simon Wiesenthal get positive press while an obsessive communist-hunter like Joe McCarthy gets vilified? Why is Marxist theory, with its alternative view of individual versus collective rights, an acceptable academic discipline, but sharia theory, with its alternative view of female empowerment, an insult to women?

The truth of the matter is that Nazism, Islamism and communism are all soul-chewing totalitarian movements. All three stand in direct opposition to Enlightenment values of rational inquiry and religious tolerance. All three seek to exterminate whoever stands in their way. Nazism justifies its genocide in the name of racial purity. Islamism, in the name of spiritual purity. Communism, in the name of socioeconomic purity.

One way or another, the shallow graves get filled.

"At the risk of seeming ridiculous," Che once wrote, "let me say that the true revolutionary is guided by a great feeling of love. It is impossible to think of a genuine revolutionary lacking this quality."

Clearly, then, Che was moved by love as he rested on top of a stone wall, chomping a cigar, commanding firing squads to take aim at rows of political dissenters . . . when he wasn't doing the honors himself. Here is Che, for example, recounting the execution of Eutimio Guerra for betraying *la Revolución*: "I fired a .32 caliber bullet into the right hemisphere of his brain which came out through his left temple. He moaned for a few moments, then died."

Here's Che in a more philosophical mode, contemplating the rule of law: "To send men to the firing squad, judicial proof is unnecessary. These procedures are an archaic bourgeois detail. This is a revolution! And a revolutionary must become a cold killing machine motivated by pure hate."

Oh, and here's Che lamenting the outcome of the Cuban Missile Crisis: "If the missiles had remained, we would have used them against the very heart of America including New York. We must never establish peaceful coexistence. In this struggle to the death between two systems we must gain the ultimate victory. We must walk the path of liberation even if it costs millions of atomic victims."

Lastly, here's Che, that paragon of revolutionary love, on his commitment to the cause: "In fact, if Christ himself stood in my way, I, like Nietzsche, would not hesitate to squish him like a worm."

Which raises an intriguing entomological question: Can a cockroach squish a worm?

"I *Still* Believe Anita Hill"

Two decades after the Senate hearings for Clarence Thomas's nomination to the U.S. Supreme Court devolved into a he-said, she-said with his former colleague Anita Hill, riveting the nation with talk of pubic hairs on Coke cans and pornographic movie stars, you have to wonder if Thomas has come to regret his actions. Surely he must realize by now that he had no right to request sexual favors from a coworker under his direct supervision . . . oh, wait, he *didn't* request sexual favors from her, according to her own testimony. But massaging her shoulders as she sat at her desk trying to do her job, *that* was clearly wrong . . . except, come to think of it, he never did that, either. He never laid a finger on her. Still, you have to feel for her, coming to work each morning, putting up with his constant requests to socialize after work . . . but that didn't quite happen, did it? Still, Thomas did make sure to keep her around the office as his personal eye candy, thwarting her professional ambitions. I mean, that's just inexcusable! Oh, wait . . . I seem to remember that he wrote letters of recommendation on her behalf and advised her on career opportunities. As a matter of fact, she *followed* him from his post at the U.S. Department of Education to his new position as head of the Equal Employment Opportunity Commission.

So let's recap, shall we?

We know that Clarence Thomas never once propositioned Anita Hill, never once put his hands on her, never hindered her employment prospects, regarded her not only as a colleague but as a protégée and a friend. We know that the sum of her accusations against him, if true, amounted to a middling case of boorishness . . . to which she never once voiced an objection, not even a casual aside, something like "Gee, Clarence, I'd really rather you didn't say stuff like that." We know that at the very moment her friend and mentor's life was subject to the glare of the national media, at the very moment his dream to serve on the Supreme Court was about to be realized, Hill came forward with stories of Thomas cracking dirty jokes, that she turned him into a late-night television punch line, and in so doing ensured that someday his obituaries will include not only the details of a distinguished career in public service and a list of principled judicial opinions but also the name Long Dong Silver.

Given the hypersexualized history of the last twenty years, it seems fair to ask whether the Thomas-Hill dustup still matters. The principals, after all, have moved on. Thomas was confirmed by the Senate, albeit narrowly, and has established a hefty legal legacy that will outlast his liberal critics. Hill emerged from the hearings as a feminist icon and has enjoyed a highly successful career as a professor of law and women's studies—so successful, indeed, given her meager scholarly output, that a cynical observer might conclude that name recognition rather than academic bona fides got her where she is. But who knows? Maybe she's a great teacher.

The deeper question, in any event, is why feminists would embrace a Judas figure like Hill as a symbol of their cause. If we're going to call a spade a spade, then there's no dodging the fact that Hill's testimony was a profound act of personal and professional betrayal—and that's assuming she was telling the truth. If she honestly believed that Thomas's behavior showed an insensitivity to women's issues and aspirations and thus rendered him unfit to serve on the Supreme Court, how could she have held her tongue and followed him when he was appointed to the Equal Employment Opportunity Commission . . . where he was specifically charged with ensuring a level playing field for women in the workplace?

What, in other words, does Anita Hill's ongoing iconic status tell us about feminism? Let's start by acknowledging the obvious: The women's liberation movement, which dates back in the United States at least to the Seneca Falls Convention of 1848, is a genuine *liberatory* movement. If you've ever asked a little girl what she wants to be when she grows up, and watched the spark come into her eyes as she conjures up her future as a veterinarian or a lawyer or a politician, you understand the immorality of a strict patriarchy. No one in his right mind wants to return America to a time in which women were limited to domestic chores, with an exception made for the occasional spinster schoolmarm—even though many contemporary feminists speak as though that's the secret fantasy of every red-blooded conservative male. Of course, this is no more true than the suggestion that every red-blooded liberal male harbors a secret fantasy to get into Sarah Palin's pants . . . which is ridiculous, given that the vast majority of gay men are liberals and thus have no interest in getting into Sarah Palin's pants, except perhaps in the most literal sense.

The main problem with feminism is that it exhausted its legitimate claims on America's conscience almost forty years ago. Feminist arguments carried the day. During a single ten-year span, from 1963 to 1973, federal legislation was passed, and legal decisions were rendered, to address current inequities and past injustices. Afterward, there was nowhere else to go . . .

Equal pay for equal work? Check, courtesy of the Equal Pay Act (1963), which outlawed wage disparities based solely on gender. Equally qualified and experienced women had to be paid the same as men for performing the same job.

Remedy for historical exclusions? Check, courtesy of Executive Order 11375 (1967), which extended the federal principles of affirmative action to include women as a favored class.

Freedom from biological determinism? Check, courtesy of the Supreme Court's ruling in *Roe v. Wade* (1973). The court rendered a woman's choice to carry her fetus to term hers alone; the state couldn't intervene on behalf of the fetus until the third trimester, or roughly the point of viability, at which time fetal rights could be taken into account. However dubious the court's reasoning, the upshot was that women now controlled the decision to bear a child—a decision with long-term career and economic consequences.

By 1973, in short, the women's movement had won federal guarantees of equal pay, slightly-more-than-equal opportunity and reproductive autonomy for every woman in the United States. The playing field was level. There was nothing left to do at that point except let nature take its course, and wait for the passage of time to dissolve the institutional advantages men had acquired over centuries.

But of course that's not what happened.

With its reasonable objectives achieved, feminism became, in effect, a movement without a cause. It mutated from a rights-driven community to a grievance-driven community, a collective whine in search of a pretext to give itself voice. (The process will be familiar to anyone who has studied the evolution of civil rights organizations over the same period.) Feminists began hitching their intellectual wagons to whatever seemed to undermine the patriarchal foundations of Western civilization. Never mind that Western civilization had given rise to the Enlightenment—without which feminism would have been unthinkable in the first place. Thus the parade of radical ideologies and outright idiocies embraced by successive generations of feminists: anarchism, communism, multiculturalism, postcolonialism, postmodernism, ethnic and gender studies, peace studies, identity politics, self-help and actualization, earth worship, goddess cults, recovered memories, sex-neutral language, campus speech codes and Take Back the Night rallies.

It's hard to overstate just how silly much of this can get. Feminist academics, for example, have argued that mathematics, physics and logic itself are tools of male oppression.[2] Relying on intuition, empathy and personal experience, by contrast, represents a more female-oriented approach to learning. No wonder, then, that our universities, steeped in patriarchal biases, have valued scientific method over feelings and anecdotes! It's just a plot to keep women out of the hard sciences! Hence, we find the renowned feminist philosopher Luce Irigaray taking issue with Einstein's math: "Is $e=mc^2$ a sexed equation? Perhaps it is. Let us make the hypothesis that it is insofar as it privileges the speed of light over other speeds that are vitally necessary to us. What seems to me to indicate the possibly sexed nature of the equation is not directly its uses by nuclear weapons, rather it is having privileged what goes the fastest. . . ."

No, she's not kidding.

Academic feminism, indeed, lacks the discipline even to be called a discipline. Rather, it has evolved into an intellectual group hug, a Gershwin refrain gone bad: *'s wonderful, 's powerful, you're anthologized!* An average Al-Anon meeting sounds like an Oxford debate compared with an average women's studies conference—which consists of a hodgepodge of free-associative verbal tics, conspiracy theorizing and a checklist of radical chic causes, held together by a congealed psychic mucus of misanthropy, misogamy and conservative-bashing, and scored by the supportive ululations of wide-eyed undergraduates.

To be fair, academic feminism is no more preposterous than several other intellectual fiefdoms of the modern American university; "feminist scholarship" is no more a contradiction in terms than, say, "Marxist thought" or "black studies." Sheltered from the outside world, and its nasty demand for reality checks, feminist professors have genuflected at the altar of relativism for four decades, oblivious to the logical corollary that if nothing whatsoever is certain, the fact of women's historical subjugation becomes just another myth. Do women have the same human potentials as men? Some "discourse communities" think they do; some think that they don't. Who are we to judge between them?

The fact that academic feminism succumbed to the terminological bluff of critical theory—seduced into irrelevancy by highfalutin gibberish—is ironic but of no great concern unless you or your loved one gets trapped in a seminar on the gynocentric dialogic. Girls just want to have fun, right? Even if it's verbal sheboppery, where's the harm?

Much more difficult to write off is the path feminism has taken beyond the ivory tower . . . and it's here that Anita Hill remains such a seminal (let it go) figure. The Thomas-Hill morality play unfolded at the nexus of three of the great subliminal fault lines of the women's movement: perpetual subjugation, racial angst and reproductive freedom.

The first is the most obvious. If women ever stop perceiving themselves as subjugated by individual men and by male-dominated society, the rationale for a women's movement evaporates. (Again, the parallels with the civil rights movement are stark.) The idea that a woman like Anita Hill—a graduate of Yale Law School and an accomplished attorney—couldn't muster the nerve to tell off her boss when faced with lewd and insulting behavior just *had* to be true because it highlights the systematic injustice of patriarchal power. If the head of the EEOC was a pig, what man wasn't? And if Hill had internalized such acquiescence, what chance did a secretary with a GED have?

The element of racial angst in the feminist embrace of Anita Hill should also be mentioned. There's no sidestepping the reality that the women's movement has traditionally been an overwhelmingly *white* women's movement. If you mute out the obligatory Aretha Franklin music, you notice that feminist rallies tend to have the color composition of polar bears in a snowstorm. To offset their collective melanin deficiency, contemporary feminists often rush to embrace any black woman who claims victimization at the hands of a man—no matter how tenuous the claim. The Duke lacrosse rape case is a more recent example. But Anita Hill remains the classic exemplar, she-who-must-be-believed. Not only because she is a black woman but because her congressional testimony was intended to submarine the Supreme Court nomination of Thomas, who feminists feared might eventually vote to overturn the *Roe* decision.

Which brings us, finally, to the issue of reproductive freedom in the feminist embrace of Anita Hill. It should be noted that the issue itself is racially fraught. Margaret Sanger, the great champion of birth control in the United States and founder of Planned Parenthood of America, was a dyed-in-the-wool, Ku Klux Klan–sympathizing eugenicist and racist. She began the Negro Project in 1939 for the express purpose of lowering birthrates among black Americans—as part of her broader goal of weeding out "inferior" human specimens. According to the Negro Project's own report, "The mass of significant Negroes still breed carelessly and disastrously, with the result that the increase among Negroes, even more than among whites, is [in] that proportion of the population least intelligent and fit."[3] Sanger recognized the explosiveness of the project's objectives and proposed, in a 1939 letter to her colleague Clarence Gamble, to recruit black clergymen to the cause: "We do not want word to go out that we want to exterminate the Negro population, and the minister is the man who can straighten out that idea if it ever occurs to any of their more rebellious members."[4]

Whatever your views on abortion as a form of birth control, there can be no doubt that the original rationale for its legalization was tinged with the racist view that dark-skinned people were less fit to survive. Nor can there be the slightest doubt that a grotesquely disproportionate number of abortions since its legalization have been provided to black women. Finally, there can be no doubt that the quest to keep abortion legal remains *the* central concern of the feminist movement in the United States.

Thus the Clarence Thomas–Anita Hill showdown still continues to excite the passions of feminists. They still *believe* Anita Hill because they still *believe in* Anita Hill. She went toe-to-toe with the patriarchy and, if nothing else, mussed its hair. But more, much more than this, she did it *her* way. She didn't fall into the phallocentric trap of constructing a reasoned case against Thomas's record of accomplishment or judicial competence. She went after him with anecdotes and feelings. She would not be silenced!

No wonder that in October 2011, to mark the twentieth anniversary of the Thomas confirmation hearings, Stephanie Schriock, president of EMILY's List, paid homage to the bravery of Anita Hill in a column for the *Huffington Post*. Why not? Membership in the group—a pro-choice, pro-Democratic political action committee that seeks to elect women to Congress—swelled by 600 percent after Hill's televised testimony in 1991. But Schriock also takes the occasion to urge eternal vigilance. Planned Parenthood, she notes, is under continuous threat from the right-wing Voldemorts of Washington. "We honor Anita Hill today, and we pledge to honor her every day until Election Day, 2012—the Year of the Woman again."[5]

Who deserves honor more than the shrinking violet who faced down the Man by stabbing him in the back?

5

Bush Derangement Syndrome

"President Bush: Hail to the Thief"

Here's a quick arithmetic problem. First, take the total number of African Americans who were registered to vote and eligible to vote in the 2000 presidential election but who were prevented from voting by operatives for George W. Bush. Got it? Next, take the total number of wives of Henry VIII of England. Got it? Now add the two numbers together. What is the grand total?

The correct answer is *six*. Henry VIII had six wives. And no African Americans who were registered to vote and eligible to vote were prevented from voting—by Bush operatives or by anyone else—in the 2000 presidential election. Zero. Not a one. *Nada.*

If you came up with the correct answer, sorry, you're no longer welcome on Liberal Island. You've been voted off. You can turn in your Kool-Aid cup on your way to the boat. So all-encompassing is Bush Derangement Syndrome among liberals that the mere suggestion that Bush won the presidency fair and square in 2000, that he didn't steal the election from Al Gore and the Democrats, triggers an intellectual gag reflex. (For the record, the Gore camp attempted to steal the election from Bush by arguing that Floridians who couldn't follow *Green Eggs and Ham*–level voting instructions and spoiled their ballots should have their screwups counted as Gore votes; the Florida Supreme Court green-lighted the effort—over the stinging dissent of its chief justice, who predicted that the Florida ruling couldn't possibly withstand the scrutiny it was sure to receive from the U.S. Supreme Court.[1] He was right; the U.S. Supreme Court put a stop to the shenanigans.) Even now, more than a decade after the Florida recount fiasco, many liberals . . . well, most liberals . . . oh, all right, every single liberal will swear on a stack of Michael Moore DVDs that the Bush team *somehow*— maybe by printing confusing ballots, maybe by rigging vote-counting machines, maybe by calling in favors among U.S. Supreme Court justices—rode into the White House by means of a bloodless coup.

But by far the most persistent and insidious claim about the 2000 election is that Bush and his Republican minions systematically disenfranchised black voters. The fact that not a single African American has ever come forward with a remotely credible account of being prevented from voting—despite desperate searches by every major news organization in the United States to track down just such a person—does not undermine the absolute certainty among liberals that it happened. *Of course it happened!* It must be true because . . . well, how could it not be true? Liberals know it's true because they've been telling themselves it's true ever since.

Witness Democratic presidential candidate John Kerry, speaking to a predominantly black congregation in a historically black church during his 2004 campaign: "In battleground states across the country, we're hearing stories of how people are trying to make it harder to even register. We're not going to let that happen because the memories of 2000 are too strong. We're not going to allow one million African Americans to be disenfranchised."

One million? How about *one?*

The term "Bush Derangement Syndrome" was coined by the conservative commentator Charles Krauthammer in a December 2003 syndicated column. Krauthammer defined BDS as "the acute onset of paranoia in otherwise normal people in reaction to the policies, the presidency—nay—the very existence of George W. Bush." The qualifier "otherwise normal people" is crucial. It would be inaccurate and inhumane to trot out BDS to explain, for example, Harry Belafonte's contention that Bush is the world's greatest tyrant and terrorist; or Janeane Garofalo's contention that Bush and Saddam Hussein represented equal threats to world peace; or Kanye West's contention that Bush doesn't care about black people. Such statements are imbecilic, of course. But the sources must be taken into account. It's not as if Belafonte's, Garofalo's or West's mental stability on topics unrelated to Bush can be taken for granted. Each one has a hold on sanity as tenuous as a November snowflake, ready to dissolve at even the slightest shift in the wind. More representative of BDS is Pulitzer Prize–winning novelist Jane Smiley's October 2005 declaration: "In a just world, [Bush, Donald Rumsfeld, Dick Cheney and Condoleezza Rice] would be taken out and shot." Nothing Smiley has said before or since approaches the Madame

Defarge—like excess of that sentiment. It's also worth noting that in the same screed-to-the-editor at Salon.com in which she proposes his execution, she matter-of-factly asserts that Bush stole the 2000 election. After too many hours thinking about Bush, gnashing her teeth and clenching her fists, Smiley simply blew a gasket. There's no other explanation.

Unfortunately, since Krauthammer's initial coinage, BDS has gone viral. It has penetrated into the cognitive marrow of ordinary liberals, and it remains there even though Bush himself has ridden off into the political sunset. Indeed, BDS has become a veritable DNA marker of the cause of leftist politics. What began as a passing derangement has mutated into living faith, complete with its own set of dogmatic articles, stations of the progressive cross, which taken together allow entrée into polite liberal conversation.

"Bush Lied. People Died."

The most famous of all BDS verbal tics is undoubtedly the bumper sticker, cum antiwar rally cry, cum Upper West Side yoga mantra, "Bush lied. People died." What do liberals believe Bush lied about? Well, in the run-up to the invasion of Iraq, he claimed that Saddam Hussein possessed weapons of mass destruction and thus needed to be removed from power. Who died? Several thousand Americans soldiers . . . and, depending on whom you believe, perhaps a million Iraqi civilians. If indeed Bush lied and a million human beings died as a result, that *would* make Bush a war criminal and would justify, or at least make comprehensible, Smiley's suggestion that he be taken out and shot.

So let's unpack the claim, shall we?

What does it mean to say that a person lied? Dictionary
.com defines *lie* as "to speak falsely or utter untruth knowingly,
as with intent to deceive." That seems straightforward enough.
Thus when President Clinton stood before the cameras and ut-
tered the immortal words, "I did not have sexual relations with
that woman, Miss Lewinsky," that would seem to qualify as a lie.
But not so fast. As we eventually learned, Clinton subscribed to
a very narrow definition of sexual relations that did not include
the act of fellatio. (Perhaps Clinton's most notable legacy consists
of hundreds of thousands of teenage boys trying to convince their
girlfriends that oral sex doesn't count as sex.) Seizing on the defi-
nitional wiggle room, Clinton's squadron of lawyers later claimed
that the president's denials—both under oath in court, and off the
cuff in public—of a sexual relationship with Monica Lewinsky,
although *misleading*, were not technically lies.

There's always a way, in other words, to claim that someone
who seems to be lying isn't lying. But let's hold President Bush to a
higher standard. No Clintonian deconstructions. Let's stick with the
dictionary definition of *lie* and the plain sense of Bush's own words.
On October 5, 2002, six months prior to the invasion of Iraq, Bush
said, "Iraq has stockpiled biological and chemical weapons and is
rebuilding the facilities used to make more of those weapons."

We now know those words to be false. Iraq had no stockpiles
of WMDs, and no evidence has ever been found that the regime
was rebuilding facilities to make them. Therefore, we are halfway
to the Dictionary.com definition of *lie*. President Bush did *speak
falsely*. All that remains is to establish that he did so *knowingly*.
Here, of course, it's helpful if you're deranged. Then you can skip
the next step and simply claim that "everyone" knew Iraq had no

WMDs—as liberal commentators are now wont to insist. If everyone knew, then Bush must have known. Ipso facto, Bush lied.

But if you're not deranged, you've got some pesky facts to overcome. Here's a partial list:

> There is no doubt that . . . Saddam Hussein has invigorated his weapons programs. Reports indicate that biological, chemical and nuclear programs continue apace and may be back to pre–Gulf War status. In addition, Saddam continues to redefine delivery systems and is doubtless using the cover of an illicit missile program to develop longer-range missiles that will threaten the United States and our allies.
>
> *—letter to President Bush*
> *signed by Senator Bob Graham (D-FL),*
> *chairman of the Senate Intelligence Committee,*
> *December 5, 2001*

> [Saddam] has systematically violated, over the course of the past eleven years, every significant UN resolution that has demanded that he disarm and destroy his chemical and biological weapons, and any nuclear capacity. This he has refused to do.
>
> *—Representative Henry Waxman (D-CA),*
> *September 10, 2002*

> We begin with the common belief that Saddam Hussein is a tyrant and threat to the peace and stability of the region. He has ignored the mandate of the United Nations and is building weapons of mass destruction and the means of delivering them.
>
> *—Senator Carl Levin (D-MI),*
> *September 19, 2002*

Iraq's search for weapons of mass destruction has proven impossible to deter, and we should assume that it will continue as long as Saddam is in power. . . . We know that he has stored secret supplies of biological and chemical weapons throughout his country.

—*Al Gore,*
September 23, 2002

We have known for many years that Saddam Hussein is seeking and developing weapons of mass destruction.

—*Senator Ted Kennedy (D-MA),*
September 27, 2002

We are confident that Saddam Hussein retains some stockpiles of chemical and biological weapons, and that he has since embarked on a crash course to build up his chemical and biological warfare capabilities. Intelligence reports indicate that he is seeking nuclear weapons, but has not yet achieved nuclear capability.

—*Senator Robert Byrd (D-WV),*
October 3, 2002

There is unmistakable evidence that Saddam Hussein is working aggressively to develop nuclear weapons and will likely have nuclear weapons within the next five years. We also should remember we have always underestimated the progress Saddam has made in development of weapons of mass destruction.

—*Senator Jay Rockefeller (D-WV),*
October 10, 2002

In the four years since the inspectors left, intelligence reports show that Saddam Hussein has worked to rebuild his chemical and biological weapons stock, his missile delivery capability, and his nuclear program. He has also given aid, comfort and sanctuary to terrorists, including al Qaeda members.

—Senator Hillary Clinton (D-NY),
October 10, 2002

Without question, we need to disarm Saddam Hussein. He is a brutal, murderous dictator, leading an oppressive regime. . . . He presents a particularly grievous threat because he is so consistently prone to miscalculation. . . . And now he is miscalculating America's response to his continued deceit and his consistent grasp for weapons of mass destruction. . . . The threat of Saddam Hussein with weapons of mass destruction is real.

—Senator John Kerry (D-MA),
January 23, 2003

Well, sure, Bush-haters will no doubt retort, *that's what Democrats were saying in 2001–2003. They were going by the same cooked intelligence that the Bush administration was using to bamboozle the rest of us.*

Unfortunately for them, there's also this:

If Saddam rejects peace and we have to use force, our purpose is clear. We want to seriously diminish the threat posed by Iraq's weapons of mass destruction.

—President Bill Clinton,
February 17, 1998

[Saddam] will use those weapons of mass destruction again, as he has ten times since 1983.

—*National Security Advisor Sandy Berger,*
February 18, 1998

We urge you, after consulting with Congress, and consistent with the U.S. Constitution and laws, to take necessary actions . . . to respond effectively to the threat posed by Iraq's refusal to end its weapons of mass destruction programs.

—*from a letter to President Clinton,*
signed by (among others) Senators Carl Levin (D-MI),
Tom Daschle (D-SD), Joe Lieberman (D-CT)
and John Kerry (D-MA),
October 9, 1998

Saddam Hussein has been engaged in the development of weapons of mass destruction technology, which is a threat to countries in the region, and he has made a mockery of the weapons inspection process.

—*Representative Nancy Pelosi (D-CA),*
December 16, 1998

Hussein has . . . chosen to spend his money on building weapons of mass destruction and palaces for his cronies.

—*Secretary of State Madeleine Albright,*
October 10, 1999

The intrepid BDS-afflicted liberal is now confronted with mental gymnastics the likes of which would send even the bendiest Mary Lou Retton wannabe to the Bengay tube. Either he has to argue (1) that the Clinton administration was cooking the intelligence the same way the Bush administration was; or (2) that Saddam *had* WMDs when he kicked out UN weapons inspectors in 1998, and that he then utilized the window of opportunity *when the inspectors were gone* to get rid of his WMDs; or (3) that, *well, err, umm, my hands are over my ears, so I can't hear you! I can't hear you! I can't hear you!*

Were there dissenters in 2003, prior to the invasion, to the common wisdom that Saddam possessed stockpiles of WMDs? Well, yes. There was Hans Blix, chief UN weapons inspector, voicing his doubts whenever a news agency put a microphone in front of his face. But his history of evaluating Iraq's WMD capacity was checkered; as head of the International Atomic Energy Agency during the 1980s, he repeatedly praised Iraqi cooperation with inspections at the very moment Saddam was building up Iraq's WMD arsenal to its highest levels. Blix's skepticism was echoed by former UN weapons inspector Scott Ritter. But Ritter's reliability was iffy was well. He'd resigned his position in August 1998, frustrated by Saddam's continuous deceptions, and by years of chasing down rumors of anthrax stored up camels' asses, convinced that Iraq still possessed WMDs. Then, *a year after he left Iraq*, he abruptly changed his mind.

No doubt Bush had heard of Blix's and Ritter's views. But does his decision to ignore their hunches and trust the detailed assessments of every major intelligence organization on the planet mean that he *knew* that reports of Saddam's WMDs were false?

If you think so, help yourself to the Thorazine.[2]

But how could the prewar intelligence about Iraq have been so wrong? As it happens, we now know the answer to this question. According to the FBI agent who debriefed Saddam shortly before his execution in 2006, *Saddam wanted the world to believe he still had WMDs*. It's a bizarre thought, to be sure, since the UN was imposing crippling sanctions on Iraq based on that very belief. But Saddam ultimately feared UN action less than he feared an attack from Iran . . . which, he calculated, would be more likely if Iran's leaders knew he no longer had WMDs.

In retrospect, Saddam's calculus looks altogether logical. He'd fought a brutal stalemated war against Iran in the 1980s and viciously persecuted Iraq's Shiite majority out of fear they might align themselves with their Shiite neighbor. More alarming still, from Saddam's standpoint, was the fact that his own military had been decimated by the 1991 conflict with the American-led coalition. If Iran did attack, he had no chance in a conventional war. His last option was a bluff: Since he *once* possessed WMDs, and the entire world knew it, he pretended he still did. He knew it would annoy America, as well as the rest of the UN Security Council, but he figured that the threat of an American invasion was less dire than the threat of an Iranian invasion. What Saddam never counted on, of course, was September 11, 2001. The 9/11 attacks were Saddam's worst nightmare because they changed the risk equation for the United States. Suddenly, the prospect of Saddam hiding WMDs went from being an ongoing nuisance to a mortal dread. What was to stop him from handing them off to Al Qaeda?

Even a minimal commitment to rational analysis and evidentiary standards, in other words, acquits Bush of bad faith in deciding to end Saddam's regime. Saddam was suspected of stockpiling WMDs for almost a decade before Bush took office and was determined to look as guilty as possible. If a guy who's been known to carry a gun is thrusting his hand in his pocket in order to look like he's carrying a gun, you can't blame the cop on the beat for believing he's carrying a gun. Or, to mix metaphors, Saddam was walking like a duck and quacking like a duck; any wonder, then, that Bush concluded he was a duck?

Nothing said above proves that the decision to invade Iraq and oust Saddam was wise. History will render that judgment over the next few decades, irrespective of the fruit fly–durable pronouncements of the editorial staff of the *New York Times*. What it *does* prove is that Bush did not lie the country into the war. He did, however, take the country to war . . . and many people died as a result. It's grisly to harp on the actual number. It's also, in a sense, beside the point since one death is too many if the war was unwise. But liberal interest groups have often treated the civilian body count in Iraq as though it were a game of Can-You-Top-This, conjuring up death totals with the scientific rigor of a Magic 8 Ball.

Perhaps the most notorious of these efforts was undertaken by the English medical journal the *Lancet*. Back in October 2006, when most media outlets were reporting the *total* Iraqi body count at 60,000–75,000, with occasional high-end estimates of 100,000, *Lancet* researchers announced that the true number of *violent deaths alone* was between 425,000 and 800,000. Taking the low-end figure, that would average out to more than 10,000 violent deaths per month for the 41 months between the March 2003 invasion and June 2006, when the *Lancet* survey ended. That's about 350 *per day*. According to the *Lancet* survey, in other words, the *average* daily death toll was higher than the highest civilian death toll ever reported by the media for a single day.

Independent analysts soon began examining the survey's methodology. They found that the *Lancet* folks had surveyed

1,849 randomly selected households, inquired about violent and nonviolent family deaths immediately before and after the American invasion, tallied the responses and then multiplied out their results by the entire Iraqi population. But how did they know the respondents weren't exaggerating the death toll? Because, the surveyors said, 92 percent of the respondents produced death certificates. Except if you multiply out the *death certificate* numbers, that means more than 92 percent of the 425,000 violent deaths would have had accompanying death certificates—that is, a minimum of 391,000 death certificates. But who issued them? Certainly not the Iraqi government, which was reporting fewer than 75,000 civilian deaths from violent and nonviolent causes combined.

In other words, the *Lancet* researchers were either dupes or propagandists. But of course the *Lancet* figures were adopted in a nanosecond by critics of the war and remained a liberal talking point until September 2007, when a British polling agency called Opinion Research Business, using similar methods to the *Lancet*'s, upped the ante to roughly one million violent deaths of Iraqi civilians.

Both the *Lancet* and ORB surveys have long since been discredited. The true body count of Iraqi civilians may never be known with any degree of certainty—though most responsible media outlets now put it at roughly 100,000. What *is* certain is that these people died because President Bush decided to invade Iraq and topple Saddam's regime.

But what was the alternative scenario? It's not as though Iraq had been a tranquil oasis before the invasion. As a matter of fact, during the 1990s, the World Health Organization claimed that 4,000 Iraqi children under the age of five were dying every month as a direct result of UN sanctions against Iraq. UNICEF put the number of dead Iraqi children at 5,000 per month. Again, that's the body count *just for children under the age of five caused by UN sanctions.*

Those UN sanctions ended once Bush removed Saddam.

Certainly, the 4,000–5,000 number was a grotesque exaggeration; Saddam's own Health Ministry was providing the raw data on which it was based. That didn't stop liberal stalwarts—knee-jerk celebrities such as Susan Sarandon, Tim Robbins, Martin Sheen, Rosie O'Donnell, Bonnie Raitt, Mike Farrell, Joan Baez, Ed Asner, Jackson Browne, Pete Seeger, Richard Dreyfuss and Richard Gere; Democratic politicians such as John Conyers, Dennis Kucinich, Barbara Lee, John Lewis, Cynthia McKinney and Debbie Stabenow; and logic-challenged commentators such as Ralph Nader, Howard Zinn, Ward Churchill, Ramsey Clark, Arundhati Roy and Noam Chomsky—from citing the figure throughout the late 1990s in order to denounce whatever aspect of corporate capitalism and American interests they'd targeted at a given rally.

Each one of the aforementioned liberal stalwarts, as you'd expect, howled in outrage at Bush's decision to invade Iraq.

Again, the WHO and UNICEF numbers were hyper-inflated. More realistic estimates range between 1,400 and 2,000 dead Iraqi children per month as a result of UN sanctions.[3] (It's good to keep such numbers in mind whenever an antiwar activist tells you that the sanctions were working, so there was no need to invade.) But even if the actual number was a tenth the WHO and UNICEF numbers, let's say 400–500 dead children per month, that still makes the worst suffering of the Iraqi people during the American occupation a humanitarian respite compared with the situation before.

So unless you're willing to concede that Iraqis were better off with hundreds, and perhaps thousands, of their children dying each month, and with Saddam's jackboot on their collective neck, and with his sadistic sons Uday and Qusay on deck, and afterward their sons, and so on, and so on, in perpetuity, then you'd have to conclude that Bush's decision to remove Saddam's regime was at least morally justifiable.

Bush didn't lie . . . and many, many Iraqis were going to die whether he invaded or not.

"Impeach Bush. Torture Cheney."

As far as I can recall, I've been tortured at least three times: There was a high school gym teacher who made my entire class stand with our arms outstretched for a half hour because one boy had giggled while he was talking. There was a camp counselor who kept dunking my head underwater after I sassed him during free swim at the bungalow colony pool. And there was a burly cop who shoved me up against a brick wall and waited for a crime victim to ID me. (The victim came by a minute later and shook her head; no, I wasn't the guy who robbed her.) There may have been other occasions, but I can't remember the specifics.

According to the 1984 United Nations Convention Against Torture, to which the United States is a signatory, torture is defined as

> any act by which severe pain and suffering, whether physical or mental, is intentionally inflicted on a male or female person for such purposes as obtaining from him, or a third person,

information or a confession, punishing him for an act he or a third person has committed or is suspected of having committed, or intimidating or coercing him or a third person, or for any reason based on discrimination of any kind, when such pain or suffering is inflicted by or at the instigation of or with the consent or acquiescence of a public official or other person acting in an official capacity.

The gym teacher, the camp counselor and the burly cop were all persons "acting in an official capacity." All caused me "pain and suffering, whether physical or mental." The pain and suffering certainly seemed "severe" to me at the time. It seems less severe now, looking back; then again, pain and suffering always seem more severe when you're undergoing it, less severe looking back.

What I'm getting at here, if you haven't figured it out by now, is that the 1984 UN Convention's definition of "torture" might have been a wee bit too broad. Think about it. By UN standards, the very act of informing a detainee that he's being detained could be construed as torture since it's likely to cause him considerable mental anguish, and that mental anguish, once the gravity of the situation sets in, might well become severe.

If you stick with the 1984 UN definition, there's no question that the United States has engaged in torture in its war against totalitarian Islam. The International Committee of the Red Cross has documented cases in which, for example, CIA interrogators twirled detainees with towels around their necks and slammed them into walls—even though, it should be noted, the towels were used to prevent whiplash and the walls were specially designed to give on impact. Detainees were also stripped naked and doused with cold water, forced to stand in stress positions, confined in coffinlike boxes, deprived of solid food for days at a time, belly-slapped and, most controversially, waterboarded.[4]

The treatment of Muslim detainees, then, was decidedly more severe than any of the instances of torture I've experienced. On the other hand, it was decidedly less severe than, say, the treatment meted out to the Scottish revolutionary William Wallace (who was drawn and quartered in 1305) or the Elizabethan dramatist Thomas Kyd (who was racked in 1593) or the Jesuit priest Edmund Campion (who was racked, twice, and *then* drawn and quartered in 1581).

Therein lies the problem. If torture is defined as "any act by which severe pain and suffering, whether physical or mental, is intentionally inflicted . . . by a public official," then the question of what constitutes torture depends, in the final analysis, on what counts as "severe." I came out of my "torture" intact, both physically and mentally. So, apparently, did the Muslim detainees mentioned in the Red Cross report. Wallace, Kyd and Campion—well, not so much. Indeed, the Muslim detainees' experience of torture tracks a lot closer to mine than to Wallace's, Kyd's or Campion's.

When liberals insist that George W. Bush authorized torture, they're right in the letter-of-the-law sense that the interrogation methods he green-lighted ran afoul of the very broad definition of torture laid out by the 1984 UN Convention Against Torture—to which, let me note again, the United States is a signatory. That makes this a rare moment in which the bumper sticker truth to which the liberal mind is drawn contains an element of correspondence-with-reality truth. But the question that must be asked is *why* Bush would attempt to skirt the provisions of a treaty approved by President Reagan. What intervening event might have colored Bush's perspective on the issue?

Hmmm.

The expression "9/11 changed everything" could itself be a bumper sticker. That is, you hear it a lot, you nod in agreement, but you don't often think through what it means. What changed on 9/11? Well, we know lots of new laws were passed under the umbrella of the USA PATRIOT Act. We know the government created the Department of Homeland Security in an effort to cut down on the red tape involved in intelligence gathering. But these crucial adjustments were just window dressing. The fundamental change brought about by the events of September 11, 2001, was a shift in our collective mind-set.

Since the end of World War II, America's national security had rested, to a substantial degree, on the belief that an outright attack on the United States would be answered by retaliation on a biblical scale. That belief, it turned out, was false. Osama bin Laden called our bluff. He hit us in a horrific way, and we didn't crack open a can of indiscriminate whup-ass. We investigated, determined who was behind the attack . . . and even once we knew it was Osama, and that he was operating out of Afghanistan, even then we didn't start incinerating cities. Instead, we demanded that the Taliban government hand him over dead or alive. In doing so, we inadvertently, and unavoidably, said to the world, "Hey, remember that whole terrible swift sword thing? We were just kidding." In effect, we provided our foreign enemies with an easy-to-follow formula for making war against America: Just work your mayhem through nonstate surrogates and, after the next 9/11, if America again connects the dots, hand over a few corpses to satisfy Washington's demand for justice.

That, by the way, is the great unspoken reason for the war in Iraq—unspoken since it would've been suicidal for Bush to mention it. Saddam was clearly the most likely candidate to capitalize on that easy-to-follow formula, despite the fact that his cash-and-carry pan-Arabism was hard to square with the wall-eyed spiritual radicalism of Osama's crowd. Still, Saddam and Osama were both consumed by totalizing visions of the future of Islamic peoples, and both saw the United States as the chief hindrance to realizing their visions. More ominously, if a freelance thug like Osama had managed to kill three thousand Americans, what might a resolute sociopath like Saddam, with the resources of an oil-drenched country, accomplish? Since we could no longer depend on the threat of a nuclear clobbering to deter him, Saddam had to be dealt with once and for all. Ousting Saddam would also present hostile regimes elsewhere with a show of American force, a signal that they might be next if they provoked us—as deterrents go, not exactly on par with the prospect of sudden annihilation, but really the best we could do. The fact that Saddam was in breach of the surrender terms that kept him in power after the 1991 Gulf War provided a useful fig leaf, acquitting us of the charge of disregarding international law.

But there was no fig leaf big enough to cover the 1984 anti-torture treaty. Bush and his advisers recognized early on that following the letter of the law would mean fighting the war with one hand tied behind their back. They also recognized that this was going to be a different kind of war, waged against a different kind of enemy, under a different set of rules than anything that had come before. The need for actionable intelligence was greater because the margin for error was nil. Think about it: At the turn of the twentieth century, a half-dozen yahoos with death wishes and the latest technology available might raze a village; at the turn of the twenty-first century, a half-dozen yahoos with death wishes and the latest technology available might reduce a major city to ashes and rattle the global economy.

That's why the Bush administration came up with the concept of "enhanced interrogation techniques." It's a god-awful euphemism but a functional one. After a series of now-declassified 2002 memos from the administration's Office of Legal Counsel, written primarily by Deputy Assistant Attorney General John Yoo and signed by Assistant Attorney General Jay Bybee, the president instructed the CIA to adopt a new definition, in effect a working definition, of torture—one that zeros in on the word *severe* in the original UN document of 1984. For physical pain and suffering to be severe enough to constitute torture, Yoo wrote, it "must be equivalent in intensity to the pain accompanying serious physical injury, such as organ failure, impairment of bodily function, or even death." Mental pain and suffering "must result in significant psychological harm of significant duration, e.g., lasting for months or even years."[5]

So the CIA went to work with a newly refined definition of torture, treating detainees in ways that might well have been illegal under the 1984 treaty. Bush himself acknowledged the ethical tightrope he was walking in a September 2006 speech in which he referred to "an alternative set of procedures" used on captured terrorist leaders. "These procedures," Bush insisted, "were designed to be safe, to comply with our laws, our Constitution and our treaty obligations. The Department of Justice reviewed the authorized methods extensively and determined them to be lawful."[6]

With that hedging 2006 concession, George Bush became indistinguishable in the liberal imagination from Vlad the Impaler.

Not to mention Caligula, Nero, Attila the Hun, Genghis Khan, Ivan the Terrible, Adolf Hitler, Pol Pot, Ayatollah Khomeini and Saddam Hussein. Torturers, all! What followed was a puppet theater of finger-wagging and a cottage industry of rush-to-print books, insisting that even if Iraq became a functioning democracy, and even if Afghanistan stabilized into a decent, governable nation, Bush must forever be seen as a moral abomination because he abandoned America's core principles. Here's a partial reading list just from 2007–2008: *The Dark Side: The Inside Story of How the War on Terror Turned into a War on American Ideals*, by Jane Mayer; *Bush's Law: The Remaking of American Justice*, by Eric Lichtblau; *Torture Team: Rumsfeld's Memo and the Betrayal of American Values*, by Philippe Sands; *Cowboy Republic: Six Ways the Bush Gang Has Defied the Law*, by Marjorie Cohn; *George W. Bush, War Criminal? The Bush Administration's Liability for 269 War Crimes*, by Michael Haas; *The Prosecution of George W. Bush for Murder*, by Vincent Bugliosi.

No one, however, worked the Torturer in Chief angle to more dramatic effect than a furious little fellow named Mark Danner, a journalism professor and essayist for the *New York Review of Books*. By copping to the use of enhanced interrogation techniques—about which, it should be noted, he'd been briefing congressional leaders the entire time—President Bush, according to the banner, "set out before the country America's dark moral epic of torture, in the coils of whose contradictions we find ourselves entangled still."[7]

Dark moral epic of torture?

Let's assume, for a moment, that the phrase has a meaning, that it's not just the heavy metal flip side of "Bright Elusive Butterfly of Love." (Never mind, by the way, that Abraham Lincoln and Franklin Roosevelt oversaw abuses of captured enemies far worse than anything alleged to have occurred during Bush's dark moral epic.) The question that must be asked is whether torture is all of a piece. Who would *you* rather be tortured by: George Bush or Saddam Hussein? Under Bush's watch, a total of three jihadist leaders thought to have actionable intelligence—including the guy who planned the 9/11 attacks and personally beheaded *Wall Street Journal* reporter Daniel Pearl—were waterboarded under strictly controlled conditions to make sure no lasting harm was done. Other prisoners were belly-slapped (again, under controlled conditions), or stripped naked in 50-degree temperatures, or made to stand up for long periods, or shaken by the collar or twirled into fake walls. One or two may even have been forced to read the *New York Review of Books*.

No hot pokers to the eyes. No yanked-out fingernails. No hands in the wood chipper.

Not much of a "dark epic," when you think about it.

Danner's conclusion, nevertheless, is equally feverish: "What we can say with certainty . . . is that the United States tortured prisoners and that the Bush Administration, including the President himself, explicitly and aggressively denied that fact."[8]

But *is* that what we can say "with certainty"? Don't the 2002 memos from the Office of Legal Counsel indicate that there was sober debate within the Bush administration as to what constitutes torture, that the president had received legal advice seeking to define the concept in a more precise way, and that he acted on that advice in the belief that he was *not* authorizing torture . . . unless, of course, he was eternally bound by the ridiculously vague definition contained in the 1984 UN Convention Against Torture? *Does* it make sense to use a single classification—"torture"—to describe crucifying a detainee, waterboarding him and shining a pen light in his face for several minutes? Do all three practices rate the same blanket condemnation?

Oh, and as long as we're on the subject, didn't Bush also explicitly state in a now-declassified February 7, 2002, memo to his cabinet and Joint Chiefs of Staff that American values "call for us to treat detainees humanely, including those who are not legally entitled to such treatment"?[9]

The Danners of the world, of course, will claim that Bush never *really* meant that detainees should be treated humanely, even though he said so in a private memo to his inner circle, which he had no reason to believe would ever be made public . . . because, of course, Danner and his ilk know what Bush was *really* thinking. It's not possible, from their perspective, that serious people in the administration were wrestling with serious ethical issues, attempting to balance a concern for basic human rights with their constitutional obligation to protect the American people.

Liberals shrug off such ambiguities. Instead, they imagine President George W. de Sade presiding over a cabinet of hand-picked Snidely Whiplashes shredding our core values for the sake of their own autoerotic amusements.

George Orwell once said of Rudyard Kipling, "He sees clearly that men can only be highly civilized while other men, inevitably less civilized, are there to guard and feed them."

Words to consider over your morning croissant.

6

=== ★ ===

The Commonweal and
the Government Teat

"Freedom Isn't Free. Tax the Rich."

I'm writing these words in midtown Manhattan, where I've lived for the majority of my adult life. Right now, New York City is in midslog, struggling through a prolonged economic downturn. Not as dire as in many other places in the United States, but we're still hemorrhaging jobs and running huge deficits. The city needs money. Lots of it, and soon. But the city also has an ace in the hole. It's where people from all over the world come to visit and shop.

Maybe it's time to play that ace.

The sales tax on goods and services purchased anywhere in the five boroughs is currently 8.35 percent. So what if Mayor Bloomberg and the City Council decided to hike the sales tax to 100 percent? Just double the price of everything. Sounds logical, on paper. Think of all the extra money the city would rake in!

Except we all know what would happen. Waves of tourists would no longer be able to afford New York City hotels; they'd spend their vacation cash elsewhere. Hordes of shoppers would no longer jam into Macy's and Bloomingdale's. It might be a boon for illegal sidewalk vendors selling designer knockoffs—but they don't pay taxes, so the city would get nothing out of it. New Yorkers themselves would immediately stop buying stuff in the city. They'd hop a Port Authority bus to shop in New Jersey, or else they'd take the Long Island Rail Road to make their purchases beyond the city limits. Why? Because the extra travel costs would pale compared with the savings in sales tax.

Raising the sales tax from 8.35 percent to 100 percent would more likely bankrupt New York City than close its budget shortfall. On the other hand, if the city raised the tax to 10 percent, you wouldn't affect people's behavior as drastically—you *might* even wind up with greater revenue. But when it comes to tax increases, there's always a point of (literally) diminishing returns.

This isn't a hard concept to grasp. Even liberals can get it. Even *actors* can get it. Back in 2009, former New York governor David Patterson was making noises about ending the 30 percent tax break for film and television companies who set up shop in the state. That was too much for überliberal actor Alec Baldwin, whose TV show *30 Rock* is filmed at Silvercup Studios in Long Island City, Queens. He warned a local news reporter that New York needed to keep the status quo. "I'm telling you right now, if these tax breaks are not reinstated into the budget, film production in this town is going to collapse, and television production is going to collapse, and it's all going to go to California."[1]

Baldwin's point was that if you take away the tax breaks—in effect, if you raise tax rates on film and television production companies—you're going to end up with less actual tax revenues coming into the state's coffers. A lower percentage of *something* is still more than a higher percentage of *nothing*.

Governor Patterson saw the light, so to speak, and extended the tax breaks through 2014.[2]

Tax *rates* and tax *revenues* are not the same thing—whether we are talking about sales taxes, business taxes or personal income taxes. The exact relationship between tax rates and tax revenues is difficult to predict. As conservative economist Arthur Laffer famously pointed out, if a government cuts income tax rates to zero percent, it will obviously collect no revenues. But if a government raises income tax rates to 100 percent, it will also end up with no revenues . . . because people will stop working if they can't keep anything they earn.[3]

Again, there is always a point of diminishing returns.

What this means, in less theoretical terms, is that raising tax rates *may* raise revenues. Or it may lower revenues. Or it may have a negligible effect on revenues. There's no way to be certain in advance because people may or may not alter their behavior in response to changes in tax laws.

Yet rank-and-file liberals continue to use the phrase "raise taxes" as if it were unproblematic, as if raising rates and raising revenues were linked in a causal chain as predictable as light and heat, gravity and acceleration, a black person getting his feelings hurt and Al Sharpton holding a press conference. Even liberals who know better, or should know better, often pretend that there's no difference between tax rates and tax revenues, and when cornered will launch into a populist Kabuki about making the rich pay their "fair share."

President Obama, for example, who's savvier than Alec Baldwin about most things, took a detour through Sherwood Forest during an April 2008 presidential debate. Moderator Charlie Gibson pointed out to candidate Obama, who'd proposed raising the tax rate on capital gains from 15 percent to as high as 28 percent, that when the capital gains tax rate was *raised* during the 1980s, the federal government collected *less* money, and when it was *lowered,* first by Bill Clinton and then by George W. Bush, the government collected *more* money. Obama's response? "I would look at raising the capital gains tax for purposes of fairness."[4]

This is the liberal leveling impulse at its worst. Cutting off your nose to spite your face may feel like a fair outcome, especially if your face has gotten under your skin. But in the realm of economics, it's always bad policy.

Furthermore, what constitutes tax *fairness?* Obama invokes the principle without ever defining the term. The top 5 percent of taxpayers in the United States hauled in 31.7 percent of the total income earned by Americans according to their 2009 returns, the latest year for which information is available. That doesn't sound very fair, does it? On the other hand, the top 5 percent of taxpayers coughed up 58.7 percent of the total income taxes collected by Uncle Sam.[5] Got that? They took home roughly 32 percent of the total but paid back roughly 59 percent. Sounds as if the top 5 percent got screwed—at least if we go by the most straightforward definition of fairness.

But that's the top 5 percent. What about the top *1* percent? You know, those despised 1 Percenters whom the 99 Percenters rail against while they're out occupying public spaces and defecating on police cars.[6] For 2009, the top 1 percent of taxpayers walked off with a hefty 16.9 percent of the total income earned by Americans. Where can I get a pitchfork? But wait . . . the top 1 percent of taxpayers also paid back 36.7 percent of total tax revenues collected by the federal government.[7]

Yikes, sounds like the 1 Percenters got screwed, too.

But that still leaves the superrich, the top tenth of 1 percent of taxpayers, the derby-hatted Garfields who earned at least $1 million according to their 2009 returns and whose *average* income was a whopping $4.4 million. You know what they're doing with all that money, don't you? Screwing the rest of us! Hoarding baby formula in their custom-designed pantries. Pumping lifesaving vaccines into their lapdogs. Driving up the price of yachts that you and I would otherwise be able to afford. Most of all, they're hiring high-powered accountants to get them out of paying their fair share of taxes. No wonder they took home 7.8 percent of the total income of all Americans and paid only. . . . No, wait, this *has* to be a misprint. It says here they paid 17.1 percent of the total federal taxes.[8]

The top tenth of 1 percent paid more than twice their fair share of taxes?

Clearly, we're going to have to redefine *fairness* if we want rich people to fork over more money. So what's fair? It's an intriguing question. We'd all agree, I suspect, that America has been very good to rich people. Maybe not as good as, say, Saudi Arabia, but rich Saudis wake up every morning on a jihadist powder keg, which has to suck some of the pleasure out of their conspicuous consumption. No, if you're rich, America is still the place to be. Right now, however, America is going through dire economic times. We're

floundering, running a budget deficit for 2010 of roughly $1.3 tril-
lion.[9] Maybe, then, we can redefine fairness as a function of collective responsibility. Rich people should pay whatever is necessary to
right the ship of state.

So let's redefine *fairness* as "the tax rate rich people need to pay
to get us out of that $1.3 trillion hole."

Now we're making progress!

The next step is to calculate what tax rate on high-income
earners will bring in an additional $1.3 trillion of revenues. Let's
start with nice round numbers. Suppose we taxed everyone who
earned more than a million dollars—that top tenth of 1 percent
of American taxpayers—at a rate of 100 percent. In other words,
let's confiscate every last penny they earn. It's not a realistic option,
of course, because, as Arthur Laffer pointed out, if you tax people
at 100 percent, they stop getting out of bed in the morning. But
this is only a preliminary thought experiment, and we're just looking for a ballpark figure in order to work our way down to more
likely scenarios.

For 2009, if you confiscated every last penny of income from
every American taxpayer who earned at least $1 million, you'd
wind up with roughly $549 billion.[10]

That's not even halfway to the goal of $1.3 trillion—the
budget deficit for 2010. Which means our thought experiment
has ground to a halt. There's no reason to go on. If a tax rate of
100 percent, which would be unworkable in any case, doesn't get
us even halfway to the target, then the target is preposterously
out of reach. Taxing rich people at a higher rate might feel good
and *might* even get us increased revenues—providing that the rate
hike doesn't drastically affect rich people's behavior. But those in-

creased revenues are going to be a drop in the bucket compared with the $1.3 trillion deficit.

America, in other words, didn't wind up in a trillion-dollar hole by taxing too little. It wound up in the hole by spending too much. Making the rich pay their "fair share" isn't going to solve the problem. Making the rich pay *more* than their fair share isn't going to solve the problem.

Cutting spending will.

"For-Profit Health Care Is Extortion"

If the Occupy Wall Street wing of the liberal nanny-state crowd posted an enemies list, among the names at the very top would be pharmaceutical giants like Merck, Pfizer, GlaxoSmithKline, Gilead Sciences, Abbott Laboratories and Bristol-Myers Squibb—companies who generate billions of dollars in income from suffering and illness, who turn tragic diseases and long-term convalescences into shareholder dividends. Health care is a *right*, according to the Occupiers. The fact that corporations seek to profit from it is further proof of the evil of capitalism.

But profit is also a great motivator. For example, each of the companies listed above has played a key role in the research and development of antiretroviral drugs that treat HIV infections and prolong the lives of AIDS patients. Would those R&D dollars have been forthcoming if corporate executives didn't know that success would earn back much more than their initial investment? Here's another way to ask the same question: What was the last medical breakthrough to come from a communist country?

Corporate greed, it would seem, has an upside.

How ironic, then, to see Occupiers commemorate 2011 World AIDS Day by marching in solidarity with HIV and AIDS patients. How many of those patients would be dead now if not for the very business model the Occupiers despise?

"Better a Bleeding Heart Than None at All"

Have you ever noticed—as the late Andy Rooney might have asked—how liberals flock to psychotherapy while conservatives by and large shun it? Several years ago I pointed out the disparity to a playwright friend of mine, who was himself in therapy, and he nodded in agreement. But then he added that it shouldn't come as a surprise since liberals tend to be much more introspective than conservatives, and thus much more connected to reality.

That's one explanation. Another possible explanation is that conservatives focus more on results than on process and are therefore more prone to question the value of hiring a dubiously qualified stranger to serve as a sounding board for your deepest fears and anxieties—especially when psychologists themselves avoid talk of curing a patient, or altering a patient's behavior, or even calling a patient a "patient," and instead focus on self-awareness as the main goal of lengthy and costly treatment.[11] Psychotherapy is kind of like renting a friend, except a friend would have an emotional stake in the outcome of your talks.

Yet another possible explanation for why conservatives tend to shun therapy is that psychologists themselves often view conservatism as a mental deficiency or disorder. As clinical psychologist and Ironshrink blogger, Shawn T. Smith, has noted, "Psychology, which is unquestionably dominated by liberals, has developed an ugly habit of falsely maligning the political right. Through respectable-looking 'research,' we sling mud with flawed data and tendentious methodology. These bogus studies build on each other to create an inbred, incoherent body of literature that will be cited with unquestioning faith by the next conservative-bashing researcher."[12]

So psychology, that most sympathetic of intellectual disciplines, hasn't been very sympathetic to conservatives. Still, conservatives seem to do all right on their own. Despite a lack of couch time, conservatives tend to be happier than liberals—a result that is either paradoxical or not so paradoxical depending on which of the aforementioned explanations you buy. According to an October 2008 survey by the Pew Research Center,[13] which correlated personal happiness and party affiliation, only 25 percent of registered Democrats self-identified as "very happy"—at the exact moment their candidate for president, Barack Obama, was taking a commanding lead in pre-election polls. By contrast, as John McCain's presidential candidacy was tanking, a full 37 percent of Republicans nevertheless counted themselves as very happy. Of course, we cannot absolutely equate Republican with conservative, or Democrat with liberal. But the 37–25 differential is large enough to allow for a bit of squishiness in the categories. What's more, the trend appears durable. Going back to 1972, regardless of the political winds, conservatives have always tested substantially happier than liberals.[14]

The question is why.

Two New York University psychologists, Jaime Napier and John Jost, believe they have the answer: Liberals are more sensitive to social injustice. "Our research suggests that inequality takes a greater psychological toll on liberals than on conservatives, apparently because liberals lack ideological rationalizations that would help them frame inequality in a positive (or at least neutral) light."[15]

Got that?

Conservatives aren't as upset as liberals by inequality because conservatives are able to *rationalize* a bad situation—that is, explain it away as the result of (let's say) individual decision making rather than the result of systematic oppression. You'd need an abacus to tally up the hidden assumptions and begged questions in the Napier-Jost synaptic waltz, and it's tough to square with the fact that conservative-headed households, on average, give 30 percent more to charity than liberal households despite the fact that conservative households, on average, earn 6 percent less per year.[16] But so be it. Let's grant Professors Napier and Jost their awkward bumper sticker of a thesis that liberals are more viscerally affected than conservatives by the hardships of others, and that such hardships cause them ongoing anxiety and discomfort. So if inequality gets under their skin, yet they're too cheap to write out a personal check, let alone to tithe, that means they depend on collective action to salve their tender psyches. They depend, in other words, on big government programs to make the occasions of their anxiety and discomfort go away. On the one hand, this would explain why liberals consistently vote for higher taxes, especially when those higher taxes are earmarked to assist the less fortunate among us. On the other hand, it would also explain why liberals cling so desperately and pathetically to the belief that such assistance works. It's an intriguing thought. Maybe liberals are hardwired to prioritize aims over outcomes. So, for instance, if a conservative dares question the effectiveness of a program like Head Start, liberals will come after him hammer and tongs: *Don't you want to give poor children a chance in life? Have you no decency?*

The conservative can site reams of data to no avail. He can quote at length from the exhaustive 2010 study by the U.S. Department of Health and Human Services: "The benefits of access to Head Start at age four are largely absent by first grade for the program population as a whole. For three year olds, there are few sustained benefits, although access to the program may lead to improved parent-child relationship through first grade, a potentially important finding for children's long term development."[17] To recap, Head Start has no lasting impact on a child's academic progress—the whole point of the program—but it *might* encourage him to snuggle more with his mom . . . at least until he's six years old.

Not a lot to show for a program costing $9 billion per year and serving roughly 900,000 students . . . or about $10,000 per student, per year.[18]

If Napier and Jost are correct, and liberals' happiness depends on alleviating socioeconomic inequality, you can understand why they'd tune out the suggestion that big government programs are wastes of time and money. Tuning out the truth, however, doesn't make it untrue. The only effective way to lift people out of poverty is for poor people to do the lifting themselves by altering their behavior. Personal responsibility, not government intervention, is determinative. It's not rocket science. The "success sequence"—finishing school, getting a job, getting married and having babies, *in that order*—largely predicts upward mobility. Ron Haskins, codirector of the Center on Children and Families at the Brookings Institution, has studied census data and arrived at a startling but sobering conclusion: "If all Americans finished high school, worked full time at whatever job they then qualified for with their education, and married at the same rate as Americans had married in 1970, the poverty rate would be cut by around 70%—without additional government spending. No welfare program, however amply funded, could ever hope for anything approaching such success."[19]

But if Haskins is right, if personal responsibility rather than big government is the key to lifting people out of poverty, where does that leave liberal politics? It is the quest for a *collective* cure for inequality, remember, that makes liberals happy, that gives their political lives meaning. Up-by-the-bootstrap solutions thus hold no interest for them. Convincing a liberal to give up on a program such as Head Start is like convincing him to give up on his pursuit of happiness. Confronting reality, under the circumstances, must indeed feel like a mugging.

To ease liberal anguish, therefore, I've decided to hang out a shingle for the next page or so; I've decided to become a psychologist. (I went to graduate school, so I'm as dubiously qualified as the next guy.) Now have a seat . . . you can choose the comfy chair or the firm couch. It's your call. But remember, every decision tells me something. Now, you say you're a liberal? Your heart bleeds for the inequality that surrounds you? Hmm, I see. When did you first notice this tendency? Think back. Close your eyes. Take your time . . . you're thinking back to third grade, to Mrs. Griffin's class. What happened? You got two gold stars on a spelling test, but Sarah, the girl sitting to your left, got three gold stars, and Tom, the boy sitting to your right, got one gold star. It seemed unfair. You wanted to take one gold star away from Sarah and give it to Tom. Or else get rid of gold stars altogether. Gold stars are stupid! Imagine a third-grade class with no gold stars. It's easy if you try.

You told that to Mrs. Griffin, too, didn't you? You went right up to her after class and told her it wasn't fair that Sarah got three gold stars and you got two and Tom got one. Then you told her that gold stars were stupid. It was the first time you spoke truth to power! Then what did Mrs. Griffin say? Wait, the memory's coming back to you. You can hear her voice, even now . . .

"But Sarah spelled all ten words right. You spelled seven of them right. Tom only spelled three of them right."

"Yes, Mrs. Griffin. But all three of us *tried*."

"But Sarah spelled all the words right. You and Tom made mistakes."

"Maybe that's because her mom and dad practiced with her."

"That doesn't matter. She spelled the words right. You and Tom didn't."

"But Tom spelled the words the way he *thought* was right. Who says what's right and wrong? What if Tom's spelling is right *to him*?"

"The dictionary tells us which spelling is right and wrong."

"But who made the dictionary? Not Tom's mom and dad."

"That doesn't matter."

"But Tom's mom and dad are divorced!"

"That also doesn't matter."

"But Tom is . . ."

"Yes?"

"You know . . ."

"Tom is what?"

"Tom is a *boy*! There, I said it. Boys aren't good at spelling. They're good at kickball and making milk come through their noses. They just can't spell as good as girls."

That was when Mrs. Griffin began to laugh, and you stormed out of the classroom. You knew then and there you could never be happy while one person got three gold stars and another got only one. That was the moment, as you look back on it now, when you became a liberal.

All right, your hour's up. You can pay the receptionist on the way out.

As much as our archetypical liberal patient . . . err, *client* . . . wants to dwell on what a nice thing she tried to do for Tom, there's also the not-so-nice thing she tried to do to Sarah. To uplift Tom, she had to take Sarah down a peg; she had to level Sarah's achievement not only with Tom's but with the rest of Mrs. Griffin's third-grade class. This is the flip side of liberalism's bleeding heart: The effort to eradicate failure is also necessarily an effort to stifle excellence. To *excel*, by definition, is to better the norm, to stand out from the crowd, to move to the head of the class. The moment you allow people to outdo their peers, you create a hierarchy of excellence.

You see this trend in public education, a field dominated by liberal thought and action. According to the Higher Education Research Institute, almost half of college freshmen nationwide now report earning grade point averages of A- or above in high school, compared with fewer than 20 percent in 1966.[20] Though this might seem a harmless exercise in ego massage, consider that as more and more students get A's, the grade becomes less and less meaningful. You get a homogenization of achievement. The legit A student becomes indistinguishable from the B- student who received an A.

So, too, teachers' unions have fought tooth and nail against virtually all merit pay initiatives—even though merit pay would mean more money for many of their members—because such initiatives would rank teachers' performances by objective criteria like students' standardized test scores or graduation rates.[21]

The unions will accept merit pay only if the rankings are based on more subjective—the preferred term is *holistic*—yardsticks like "peer review" and "professional development." The suggestion that a teacher might be excelling at his job, or even that any teacher might be *objectively* outperforming any other is, well, rude. But it's more than rude. It's *illiberal*.

Liberals have been at war with excellence since at least the late 1960s. Not in their own minds, to be sure; in their own minds, they're at war with self-interest. That doesn't mean that every liberal is a closet Marxist, but I've yet to meet one who doesn't harbor a collectivist streak—who isn't convinced that pulling together with your neighbors is a finer impulse than (literally) minding your own business. The community comes before the self; that's the essence of collectivism. But self-interest is the fuel of excellence, and society as a whole profits from its expression. As the eighteenth-century Scottish economist Adam Smith said, "In competition, individual ambition serves the common good." But the principle is much older. It has been part of the American experience since the Pilgrims first landed on Plymouth Rock. The Pilgrims tried early on to set up a true collectivist society—a God-marinated version of "from each according to his abilities, to each according to his needs." It didn't work. William Bradford, the leader of the Pilgrims, wrote in 1623 that a corn shortage soon compelled them to rethink their communal ideal; it was decided that "they should set corn every man for his own particular, and in that regard trust to themselves." The new arrangement, according to Bradford, "had very good success, for it made all hands very industrious."[22]

What Bradford and the Pilgrims discovered in the early 1620s, and what the world would rediscover, again and again, at horrific costs, throughout the twentieth century, is that people never work as hard for an ideal, no matter how noble, as they do for themselves. No one strives to excel unless his excellence is recognized and rewarded. That's the nature of self-interest. That's also human nature.

Maybe, then, the reason liberals are not as happy as conservatives has less to do with an aversion to inequality than with an aversion to human nature.[23] Maybe it's not the socioeconomic gap between the haves and have-nots that is so upsetting to liberals but rather the unseemly spectacle of people striving to outdo one another. Maybe liberals just take a dimmer view of mankind than conservatives do . . . which, of course, would account for why liberals donate less than conservatives to organized charities but, at least in my experience, are more likely to hand a dollar to a bum on the street. Maybe, like Jonathan Swift, liberals "hate and detest that animal called man" but "heartily love John, Peter, Thomas and so forth."

You can understand, even admire, the sentiment. You just don't want anyone who feels that way to make public policy.

"Homelessness Isn't a Choice: It's a Crime Against Humanity"

Scenes from midtown Manhattan, early twenty-first century:

- Wednesday night, around eight-fifteen, a guy is leaning into a green trash bin on Broadway. His two feet are off the ground. He's flinging trash out behind him onto the sidewalk, scouring the refuse for plastic bottles and aluminum cans. He stops long enough to ask you if you can help him out. When you answer no, he returns to his search. In the distance, half a dozen black garbage bags are torn open, their contents strewn from the curb to the plaza of a high-rise office building.

- Friday morning, eleven-thirty, the downtown local subway pulls into the station at Seventh Avenue and Fiftieth Street. The first car is, surprisingly, half empty. You step inside and discover a guy sleeping on his side at the front of the car; thirty other riders are jammed together at the rear of the car. The reason for the gap becomes clear as soon as you inhale. The stench coming off the sleeper would gag a skunk.

- Sunday afternoon, at four-thirty, the subway entrance at Thirty-Fourth Street and Herald Square is jammed as you approach. The crowd is backed up six deep at the first step. The stairwell below is divided by a metal banister; it's supposed to separate commuters exiting the station from commuters entering the station, but the entire right half of the stairwell is taken up by a morbidly obese woman lying across the third step from the bottom, holding out a paper cup for change, moaning, *"Pleeeeeease."*

- Tuesday night, ten-fifteen, you're weary from a long day of work but decide to stop for cash at an ATM machine on Madison Avenue. You're let inside by a guy who'd need a two-week makeover to be described as "disheveled." The guy halfheartedly asks you for change but then hustles off without even waiting for an answer. The reason for his haste becomes apparent an instant later. He's defecated in front of the last ATM.

- Wednesday afternoon, around twelve-fifteen, a guy is muttering to himself, weaving back and forth along the sidewalk on Forty-Eighth Street, pausing now and then to rip loose-hanging vines out of the decorative planters in front of a residential building. He crosses paths with a young woman walking her Chihuahua; the dog barks playfully at him. He lunges at the dog and attempts to kick it, but the Chihuahua jumps backward and eludes him. Both dog and owner scurry away as the guy resumes his weaving and ripping tour up the block.

Now, of course, it's considered bad form to criticize people who are down on their luck . . . except the very phrase "down on their luck" assigns a far greater role to chance than the evidence bears out. According to a 2009 survey by the U.S. Department of Housing and Urban Development, 43 percent of the homeless have a disability.[24] But this is a deeply dishonest statistic, and for at least two reasons: In the first place, it reflects the liberal penchant for leveling conditions and circumstances by blurring natural distinctions; thus blind people and amputees are grouped with crackheads and drunks under the umbrella term *the disabled homeless*. But crackheads and drunks wake up every morning with a chance to put down the pipe or cork the bottle. The blind can't put on their bifocals, and amputees can't regrow their limbs. In the second place, the HUD number doesn't address the issue of how many *physically* disabled homeless acquired their disability by way of a behavioral disorder. How many blind homeless people went blind via macular degeneration due to alcoholism? How many amputees lost their limbs through gangrene caused by excessive smoking or drinking? Left unanswered in the HUD survey, in other words, is the relationship between bodily disability and behavioral disability among the homeless.

More to the point is a recent assessment by the ultraliberal National Health Care for the Homeless Council. (Their slogan:

Because Health Care Is a Right, not a Privilege.) According to NHCHC, "Approximately one-third [of homeless people] have mental illnesses. Perhaps one-half have a current or past drug or alcohol addiction."[25] Even allowing for a significant overlap between the one-third who are deranged and the one-half who are addicted, you're still looking at a likelihood—maybe a two-thirds likelihood—that the homeless guy you encounter on your daily commute is either out of his mind at that moment or is attempting to get out of his mind as soon as possible.[26]

The fundamental truth about the homeless is that they are decidedly *not* like you and me. Homelessness doesn't strike at random; it's not an airborne contagion that can take down anyone at any moment. Nor does it happen to large numbers of people suddenly—despite hysterical headlines in liberal publications to that effect: "One Third of Americans One Paycheck Away from Homelessness."[27] Look below the boldface and you discover that the article refers to the (far-fetched) possibility of one-third of Americans losing their homes to foreclosure, not to one-third of Americans living out on the streets.

So let's do a bit of language policing. If we're going to call people who lose their homes to foreclosure *homeless*, which makes perfect sense, then let's call people who choose to live on the streets *bums*. It's a harsher term but a more accurate one. People who choose to live on the street make that choice in order to bum cash—or booze or smokes or, on rare occasions, food—from passersby. Bums bum. That's what logicians call a tautology.

Nor can there be the slightest doubt that living on the streets is indeed a choice—as the courageous reportage of Heather Mac Donald proved in New York City in the late 1990s and 2000s. Mac Donald endured charges of heartlessness, victim-blaming and (of course) racism when she began writing about the bum lifestyle for *City Journal* and the *New York Post*; she was repeatedly heckled and shouted down at public forums when she tried to present her evidence.

The first question Mac Donald addressed was the most obvious one. Given the more than adequate shelter system available to bums, why do they stay out on the street? Advocates for the homeless claim the shelters aren't safe. But, as Mac Donald pointed out, "Street living is hardly peaceful. Bums are forever beating and stealing from each other; violence between the sexes is particularly acute."[28] But let's suppose for a moment—contrary to reality—that the shelters *aren't* safe. Wouldn't it be the occupants themselves who make them unsafe? "If the homeless are a danger to each other, why should they be allowed to occupy the streets— and put the public's lives in danger, too?"[29]

Yet in fact the shelters *are* safe. They were safe when Mac Donald was writing about them and remain safe today. The three F's of street life—fighting, falling and freezing—take the greatest toll on bums' health, not their occasional overnight stays under the supervision of social workers.[30] So if it's not a question of personal safety, why do bums prefer to sleep on subway grates and eat out of trash cans rather than accept a free bed and warm food? The answer's not hard to figure out . . . but you have to think like a bum to get it. So let's say you're a bum. That means you're likely either crazy or chemical-dependent or both. If the former, you don't want to leave the street because that's where you meet up with your imaginary playmates. If the latter, you don't want to leave the street because that's where you score your booze and dope. In either case, you don't want to leave the street because you're a bum, and that's where you do your bumming.

Here's the sad truth: If you set up every bum in Manhattan in a penthouse apartment on Park Avenue, then installed a spigot of cash over the kitchen sink, the overwhelming majority of them would wind up living on the street again because that's where their pathologies reside.[31]

Bums *want* to live on the street.

Communities don't want them there.

America's homeless dilemma boils down to a tension between the individual rights of bums and the collective rights of communities. That's it. That's the crux of problem. It has nothing to do with economic policy or with income distribution. It's not a crisis of capitalism—though, of course, liberals want to believe it's a crisis of capitalism because they *always* want to believe capitalism is in crisis. On the other hand, it is a *phenomenon* of capitalism in the sense that capitalist societies tend to maximize personal liberties. Capitalism cannot function collectively or effectively unless people are guaranteed the right to capitalize on their individual ambitions and talents.

But that guarantee has a flip side. If you have a right to capitalize on your innate qualities, you also have the right to squander your innate qualities . . . indeed, you have the right to screw up your life. "Homelessness isn't a choice," according to the bumper sticker. There's a measure of truth in that. No one *plans* to be homeless. But homelessness is one possible outcome of the freedom to choose. The freedom to choose carries with it the freedom to choose badly, the freedom even to fail miserably. As much as liberals want to pretend otherwise, failure isn't a disease. It's a reality of the human condition. In the exceptional case of homelessness, it's a bona fide lifestyle, a long pattern of failed decision

making—often rooted in psychosis or chemical dependency—
that ends in personal disaster.

You want to solve homelessness? It's not hard. You just have
to strip people of their basic autonomy: Institutionalize the crazies
and lock up the crackheads. Long term, you need to direct children from kindergarten onward into fields suited to their measur-
able aptitudes. *So little Yolanda wants to be an astronaut? Ooh, sorry
about that. Her test scores tell us she's better suited to be a bank clerk.
Here's a lovely fountain pen for her, and thanks for playing. What?
She'll be heartbroken? Ah, well, if the disappointment drives her to
drugs and alcohol, we can always haul her off later in life.*

Voilà! No more homelessness.

Except there's that pesky life-liberty-and-the-pursuit-of-
happiness thing . . .

Since stripping people of their autonomy isn't a viable option,
what remains is to find a reasonable equilibrium between the
rights of bums and the rights of communities. To what extent
should bums be allowed to inconvenience, intimidate and appall
the rest of us? Granted, it's not a nice question. It doesn't make us
feel warm and cozy inside. But it's a necessary question.

Even *asking* such a question is liable to get you called a fascist
by any liberal within earshot. Tongue-lashings, of course, are easy
enough to ignore. But a more serious and temperate concern is
that all people, including bums, have a right to use public spaces
as long as they're not harming themselves or others, so the rest of
us just have to put up with their adventures in degradation.

Maybe so.

But *harm* can be psychological as well as physical. The courts,
for instance, recognize mental anguish as a rationale for second
trimester abortions. The Internal Revenue Service permits us to

deduct psychotherapy bills from our taxes. Insurance companies cover antidepressant drugs. Yet the reality of psychological harm seems to fade, at least in liberals' minds, when weighing the rights of the public versus the rights of public nuisances. Even supposing that only one in a thousand bums would ever, let's say, crush the skull of a passerby with a brick, the possibility that the obscenity-muttering, filth-encrusted guy on the corner might be that one is a source of daily tension in city life.

Civil society, moreover, is founded on the principle of reciprocal obligations. In exchange for the benefits and protections of the state, individuals surrender certain liberties to the collective good. Even though, on occasion, I might *want* to drive 100 miles per hour, I can't—the loss of which liberty is compensated by my not being endangered by other people driving 100 miles per hour.

Likewise, my right to use a public space depends on my not unduly hindering its use by others. So, for example, I'm free to sell my wristwatch on the corner because the inconvenience to passersby is minimal; I cannot, however, drag my sofa onto the sidewalk and auction it off to the highest bidder because I'd drastically obstruct pedestrian traffic.

Bums, no more or less than mailroom clerks or corporate CEOs, are implicitly bound to observe commonsense standards of conduct in public spaces. To argue that they cannot recognize such standards owing to their diminished capacity is, in effect, to argue for their forcible removal. The suggestion that they shouldn't be blamed for behavior that would be blameworthy in housebroken pets serves only to dehumanize them further.

Civil society has a right to demand civility.

7

━━ ★ ━━

Bêtes Noires

"Shame on Israel"

On May 2, 2004, an Israeli social worker named Tali Hatuel, who was eight months pregnant, was driving from central Israel to her home in the settlement town of Gush Katif on the Gaza Strip. Riding with her were her four daughters: eleven-year-old Hila, nine-year-old Hadar, seven-year-old Roni and two-year-old Merav. Two Palestinian gunmen opened fire on the passing car, wounding Tali and forcing the car from the road. The gunmen then rushed the car and discovered that the driver was a pregnant woman—at which point they pumped bullets into her abdomen and face . . . and then pumped bullets into the face of her eleven-year-old daughter . . . and into the face of her nine-year-old daughter . . . and into the face of her seven-year-old daughter . . . and into the face of her two-year-old daughter. The gunmen were later found and killed by Israeli Defense Forces. The next day, two

Palestinian organizations, Islamic Jihad and the Popular Resistance Committee, both claimed credit for the attack, and state-sponsored Voice of Palestine radio called it a "heroic operation."[1]

One week after the ambush, there was a memorial service for Tali Hatuel and her daughters. Two more Palestinian gunmen, dressed in women's clothing, came up behind the mourners, including women and young children, and opened fire. They missed their targets this time and were shot dead by Israeli soldiers who were providing security at the event. Islamic Jihad and the Popular Resistance Committee again claimed credit for the follow-up attack.

Liberals, of course, will caution us against judging Palestinians based on . . . well, based on what they do. Pay no attention to those Palestinian youths caught on video smearing their hands with the blood of a murdered Israeli border guard and waving them to a cheering mob. Forget about those Palestinian parents weeping with pride at their teenage son's suicidal massacre of Jewish teenagers. Never mind that Palestinian toddler dolled up in a mock explosive vest and paraded by friends and family before TV cameras.

No, liberals insist, we shouldn't judge Palestinians on their actions. Because Palestinian actions are always just *re*actions. They gun down women and children and blow themselves up in markets and pizza parlors the way ragged claws scuttle along the floors of silent seas; it's not as though they *mean* to do it. Liberals remind us that Palestinians have been living under Israeli occupation since 1967, and that they were wronged by the creation of a Jewish state in their midst in 1948, so we mustn't hold them morally responsible for attacks like the one on the Hatuel family. Or for the claims of credit that followed. How could they help themselves, really? It was Israel's own oppressive policies, when you stop and think about it, that killed Tali Hatuel and her daughters.[2] That's the mind-set of Israel's liberal critics. Which raises an intriguing metaphysical question: How much oppression would *you* have to endure before you'd shoot a cowering two-year-old in the face? How much before you'd applaud your neighbor's decision to take that shot?

Historical context is always worth keeping in mind, but in this case you don't need to wade too far into the six-decades-and-counting Israeli-Palestinian struggle to sort out the good guys from the bad guys. You can only focus on the dog whistle of real and imagined grievances for so long before you confront the game-set-match recognition that one side, with the ability to decimate its enemy, seeks to avoid conflict and, when provoked, minimize nonmilitary casualties, while the other side conducts a relentless campaign of gunfire and bomb and rocket attacks designed to maximize nonmilitary casualties. One side exchanges land for peace—even though it never gets peace in return—and deploys its soldiers, in uniform, to defend its shrinking territory against sudden violence; the other side trains civilians to act as human bombs and cannon fodder, targets civilians throughout the territory of its enemy and hides among civilians when its enemy retaliates.

To deny, under the circumstances, that the first side has the moral high ground is to check your prefrontal lobe at the front door. Until the Israeli Air Force starts turning Palestinian towns on the West Bank and Gaza Strip into miniature Dresdens, circa 1945, no reasonable observer can fault Israel's forbearance.

The problem, however, is that many of Israel's fiercest critics don't qualify as reasonable observers. They tend to be culled from two of the knee-jerkiest groups of people on earth, college faculty and college students, whose capacity for rational analysis has either been snuffed out by the bizarro groupthink of academia or severely retarded by twelve years of multicultural mush. To be reasonable, in their universe, is the *last* thing you'd want to be. To be reasonable is to be detached. How can you remain detached when people are dying? To be committed, really and truly committed, you need to follow your gut! And their guts have been roiled by dozens of photo ops of Palestinian youth hurling rocks at Israeli tanks, then marinated in a campus cauldron of crypto-Marxist cant about exclusion and exploitation. On a gut level, they sense that the struggle between the Palestinians and Israel boils down to a clash between the powerless and the privileged, between teenagers with slingshots and soldiers with rifles, between David and Goliath. How can Goliath ever have the high moral ground?

Here, again, liberals are seduced by the worst foolishness of Romanticism, reflexively painting halos over anyone and anything that rejects the intellectual and cultural institutions of Western civilization. The Palestinians are a primitive desert people whose sincere wish is to live the same ignorant, squalid, Jew-hating lives their ancestors did a millennium ago. That's their heritage, their golden age. All that's stopping them from recapturing it is the natural resource–poor, indoor plumbing–rich nation of Israel.

This isn't to say that the Palestinians haven't gotten screwed over for the last century . . . mostly by the Hashemite Dynasty of Jordan, whose nation now sits on much of the land covered by the 1922 British mandate for Palestine. It was the British mandate that divvied up the region between Jews and Arabs. During the 1948–49 Arab-Israeli war, in which Israel first declared its independence and then repelled attacks from its Arab neighbors, the Hash-emites under King Abdullah gained control of the West Bank, home to roughly half a million Palestinian Arabs.[3] Abdullah, who envisioned a pan-Arabian kingdom with himself on the throne, held on to the West Bank and its Palestinian population under the terms of the 1949 peace treaty between Israel and Jordan. The Second Arab-Palestinian Conference, held in December of that year, proposed a unified Jordan consisting of both Hashemites and Palestinians, and the unification was formally approved by the Jor-danian National Assembly and Abdullah in 1950.

That should have been the end of Palestinian miseries, or at least the start of the end. Indeed, the unification of the West Bank and Jordan made the Palestinians a majority of the total Jordanian population. Though still ruled by the Hashemite mi-nority, the Palestinians were no longer stateless. But Jordan, along with Egypt, Syria and Iraq, provoked another war with Israel in 1967—one that lasted all of six days. That war left Israel in control of the West Bank and Gaza Strip, which Israel decided to keep as a buffer zone against future Arab invasions . . . even though the lands were home to many Palestinian Arabs.

Predictably, the Palestinians who remained in Jordan were not pleased to be severed from their brethren. They blamed Israel, of course, but also the Hashemite rulers of Jordan. Greater repres-sion followed, with the Hashemites worried that the Palestinians in their midst would seek autonomous rule. Fighting erupted in the early 1970s between Palestinians and Hashemites, which ended with the expulsion of large numbers of Palestinians from Jordanian territory.

With their political prospects in Jordan dashed, the Palestin-ians were able to focus the totality of their discontent and violence on Israel. Focus it they did, for four decades and running. They've decided that the land of Israel—"from the river to the sea," as pro-Palestinian demonstrators like to chant—is their eternal home-land. Not Jordan. Not the West Bank and Gaza. Every square inch of territory from the Jordan River to the Mediterranean Sea. It's their divine right. All that has to happen is for the Jewish state to cease to exist. That's the Palestinian dream, and, if we take them at their words, it's not negotiable.

It ain't gonna happen.

But surely, liberals insist, there must be a fair compromise. There's *always* a fair compromise. Except when the Palestinians' persistent, heartfelt, life-defining demand is for the world to rec-ognize their divine right to possess the entirety of the land that now makes up Israel—in effect, to drive the Jews into the sea—what would a fair compromise look like? Jews agreeing to be driven into the sea up to their waists?

The only good Israeli is a wet Israeli?

"Fox News—Terrorist News Network"

Fox News tilts to the right. There, I've said it. The network tilts to the right not only in its evening lineup of opinion programs but also in its hard news coverage during the day. No fair and balanced observer can fail to observe that Fox tends to trumpet stories that make liberal politicians and causes look bad and downplay stories that make conservative politicians and causes look bad.

Does Fox News tilt further to the right than its direct com-petitors, CNN and MSNBC, tilt to the left? That's hard to say. (I'm skipping the nightly newscasts on ABC, CBS and NBC here out of respect for the dead.) Different studies have come to diametrically opposite conclusions, and the methods for detecting bias tend to be so squishy that the studies themselves remain open to accusations of bias. If, for example, Fox runs more stories than either CNN or MSNBC questioning whether climate change is caused by human activity, does that make Fox more slanted or CNN and MSNBC more gullible?

Are Fox viewers less informed, or more misinformed, than viewers of other news networks—as the comedian Jon Stewart fiercely (almost demonically) insisted in a notorious 2011 interview with Fox News anchor Chris Wallace? Again, the answer depends on which survey you trust . . . as Stewart himself was forced to concede after his rant. And, again, the issue of methodology is unavoidable. Fox viewers, for example, are more likely than viewers of CNN or MSNBC to believe that Saddam Hussein was involved in the attacks of 9/11. He wasn't. So if that's your informational yardstick, Fox viewers look misinformed. But what if your yardstick is the belief that President Bush actually claimed that Saddam was involved in 9/11? The fact that he didn't, not even once, will come as a shock to many viewers of CNN and MSNBC.

The level of Fox's bias is therefore open to debate. The level of animus Fox inspires in its competitors is not. Former MSNBC lead anchor Keith Olbermann once told *Playboy* magazine,

> Al Qaeda really hurt us, but not as much as Rupert Murdoch has hurt us, particularly in the case of Fox News. Fox News is worse that Al Qaeda—worse for our society. It's as dangerous as the Ku Klux Klan ever was.

Olbermann, of course, was MSNBC's longtime standard bearer in its hapless quest to cut into Fox's prime-time audience and is a fascinating case in his own right. The critical point to keep in mind about Olbermann is that he got his big media break as a baseball card maven and has always been a jock-sniffer at heart, a refugee from ESPN's *SportsCenter* who waded into the deep end of the cable news pool buoyed by the belief that you can use exclamation points to tighten a syllogism. Charismatic in the way that spectacularly callow people often are, he brought to nightly news commentary the rhetorical method of the average sports debate: *You-can-tell-I'm-right-because-I'm-more-worked-up-than-you-are*. But the very fact that he reasons in the imperative mode—Impeach! Indict! Resign!—put him at the epicenter of a genuine liberal zeitgeist in the waning years of the Bush administration, the perfect hyperventilating embodiment of Bush Derangement Syndrome:

I accuse you, Mr. Bush, of lying this country into war. I accuse you of fabricating in the minds of your own people a false implied link between Saddam Hussein and 9/11. I accuse you of firing the generals who told you that the plans for Iraq were disastrously insufficient. I accuse you of causing in Iraq the needless deaths of 3,586 of our brothers and sons, and sisters and daughters, and friends and neighbors. I accuse you of subverting the Constitution, not in some misguided but sincerely motivated struggle to combat terrorists, but to stifle dissent. I accuse you of fomenting fear among your own people, of creating the very terror you claim to have fought. I accuse you of exploiting that unreasoning fear, the natural fear of your own people who just want to live their lives in peace, as a political tool to slander your critics and libel your opponents. I accuse you of handing part of this Republic over to a vice president who is without conscience, and letting him run roughshod over it.

You'd need a tick sheet to keep track of the begged questions, hyperbolic claims and outright non sequiturs in such a passage. Except Olbermann isn't really *reasoning*; he's *accusing*. Plus, his voice has dropped an octave, so you know he's got gravitas. Logic be damned.

Olbermann's seething hatred for Bush, Cheney and company made his show comically addictive—in much the same way that America's Wildest Car Chases is comically addictive. But its amusement value was also offset by his creepy fixation with his eight o'clock rival on Fox, Bill O'Reilly. Olbermann taunted him on a nightly basis with schoolyard variants of his name like *Bill-O the Clown* and *Oh-Really?*; he devoted long swathes of airtime to chronicling O'Reilly's slightest gaffes and invented his signature segment, "Worst Person in the World," as a pretext to take a shot at O'Reilly whenever possible.

For his part, O'Reilly never even mentioned Olbermann by name.

The Olbermann-O'Reilly one-way feud is thus emblematic of the obsession-revulsion that Fox News excites in its competition. Fox is like that head cheerleader the other high school girls call a tramp while they're copying her wardrobe. They detest her in that special foot-stamping, early-menstrual way. The more they detest her, the more they can't take their eyes off her.

But why is Fox so successful?

One obvious reason is that Fox executives know what makes engaging TV, as their ratings dominance night after night underscores. Hosting an hour-long political program five times per week means repeating yourself ad nauseam, trafficking in multiple clichés, provoking occasional controversies, devising corny comic bits and inoffensive filler segments and developing a stable of reliable guests adept at keeping things moving but not rocking the boat. That's the formula. Its competitors understand this as well as Fox does. But Fox recruits hosts who are exceptionally good at it . . . and who are also exceptionally durable. O'Reilly has hosted *The O'Reilly Factor* since the launch of Fox News in October 1996. Sean Hannity came on board at the start, too, cohosting *Hannity & Colmes* with liberal commentator Alan Colmes until January 2009, at which point Colmes left, and the show was renamed *Hannity*. Greta Van Susteren slid into the ten o'clock slot in 2002 with *On the Record* to fill out Fox's 8–11 p.m. prime-time block. The O'Reilly–Hannity–Van Susteren lineup has held ever since. With the exception of CNN's apolitical *Larry King Live*, which folded its tent in 2010 after twenty-five years on the air, neither of Fox's main cable rivals has been able to sustain a prime-time program as long as *On the Record*.

So Fox's keen eye for on-air personalities is one reason for the network's prime-time supremacy. But it can't be the only reason. Olbermann, after all, was a definite talent—albeit in a *yikes* kind of way. Yet he couldn't dent the Fox juggernaut. Neither could Rachel Maddow, who took a brainier, more sardonic, and less self-righteous approach than Olbermann . . . even though, it should be noted, she once lectured former secretary of homeland security, Pennsylvania governor, six-time congressman, Vietnam veteran and Bronze Star recipient Tom Ridge on his naïveté for believing that the decision to invade Iraq was made in good faith by the Bush administration. (If sheer hubris equated with viewership, her numbers would've shot through the roof.)

For years now, MSNBC has attempted to structure, and re-structure, and then re-restructure its nighttime lineup around the theme "Look at what doody-faces those Republicans are!" It's lowbrow, to be sure, but there *should* be an audience for it, given the fifty-fifty split of the electorate and the partisan rancor of the current political climate. But its ratings languish.

Perhaps, though, MSNBC's main problem isn't Fox News but CNN. The latter's left-of-center bias isn't as in-your-face as MSNBC's—that is, it doesn't rise to the level of a raison d'être—but the bias is there. Wrapping up a straight news report about a 2006 meeting between British prime minister Tony Blair and President Bush, CNN *correspondent* (not commentator) Suzanne Malveaux once declared,

> [Bush and Blair] have stood shoulder to shoulder on the Iraq war since the very beginning, critics calling Mr. Bush "the cowboy" for stubbornly leading the charge, and Mr. Blair "the poodle" for obediently following. But three years since the U.S. invasion, the two are still adamant that their Iraq mission is sound. President Bush didn't just drink the Kool-Aid, he made it. But perhaps now it's a little less sweet.

Still, in the realm of CNN knee jerks, it would be difficult to top Wolf Blitzer's classic descent into liberal pathos in the aftermath of Hurricane Katrina, as he reported on the plight of New Orleans residents: "You simply get chills every time you see these poor individuals . . . almost all of them that we see are so poor, and they are so black, and this is going to raise lots of questions for people who are watching this story unfold."

How black were they, Wolfie? Oh, and what questions— *nudge, nudge*—do you have in mind?

Here, then, we come to the likeliest, Occam's razor explanation of Fox News' ongoing domination of its cable rivals: *It has no competitors for conservative viewers.* Think about it. If you're a liberal, and you like your news televised and tilted, you've got a rich buffet of cable and broadcast sources to choose from every night, ranging from a gentle leftward lean to *Pravda*-without-the-accents. (Here you can include the dead-broadcast-transmitting nightly half hours on ABC, CBS and NBC—which have leaned decidedly leftward since at least the Vietnam era, and, in the case of CBS, going back to the Army-McCarthy hearings.) But if you're conservative, there's nowhere to turn except Fox without having your opinions, indeed, your perception of reality, sneered at.

Fox's success, in other words, is a roundabout confirmation of the liberal bias of the rest of television news . . . which, in a final irony, many liberal viewers still regard as a myth. But it is no myth.

Testament to it is the "fair and balanced" bitch slap to which Fox's rivals are subjected in the ratings.

"Sarah Palin, Hero of the Stupid"

Here's a quick *Jeopardy* challenge. The category is recent political gaffes:

1. During prepared remarks in which he proposed new financial regulations, this politicians stated, "Even as we

dig our way out of this deep hole, we must not lose sight of what led us into this mess." *A year later*, he was still obliviously using the dig-ourselves-out-of-a-hole metaphor. [Answer: Who is Barack Obama?]

2. While campaigning for the Senate, this politician once recounted events from the life of Harriet Tubman thinking she was giving an inspirational talk on the life of Sojourner Truth. [Answer: Who is Hillary Clinton?]

3. During an overseas press conference, this politician said, "It was also interesting to see that political interaction in Europe is not that different from the United States Senate. There's a lot of—I don't know what the term is in Austrian—wheeling and dealing. . . ." [Answer: Who is Barack Obama?]

4. During a campaign speech, this politician declared that the number-one challenge facing the American economy was a "three-letter word. Jobs. J-O-B-S. Jobs." [Answer: Who is Joe Biden?]

5. During a campaign speech, this politician stated, "It's wonderful to be back in Oregon. Over the last fifteen months, we've traveled to every corner of the United States. I've now been in fifty-seven states. I think [I have] one left to go—Alaska and Hawaii." [Answer: Who is Barack Obama?]

6. In prepared remarks on the floor of Congress in 2010, this politician stated, "Today we have two Vietnams, side by side, North and South, exchanging and working." [Answer: Who is Representative Sheila Jackson Lee (D-TX)?]

7. This politician once pointed out, "Those who survived the [1989] San Francisco earthquake said, 'Thank God, I'm still alive.' But, of course, those who died—their lives

will never be the same." [Answer: Who is Senator Barbara Boxer (D-CA)?]

If you put a microphone in front of a politician's face often enough, sooner or later you're going to record a gaffe. That's the way things work. But some gaffes are written off as mere lapses, the result of fatigue or momentary confusion, while others are taken as true indicators of mental deficiency. So, for example, when Sarah Palin mashes together the words *refute* and *repudiate* and comes up with *refudiate*, it's not taken as a slip of the tongue but as another indication of her stupidity.

With the possible exceptions of George W. Bush and Dan Quayle, no politician in recent memory has had his or her intelligence mocked as often as Sarah Palin has. But in the cases of Bush and Quayle, you're dealing with a two-term president and a one-term vice president of the United States. In Palin's case, you're dealing with a *half-term* governor of Alaska who, *for three months*, was a *candidate* for vice president.

As I write these words, Palin holds no elective office. Nor is she running for an elective office. She's a private citizen who travels around the country, giving folksy, inspirational speeches for partisan causes. Yet the liberal media, and liberals in general, cannot seem to let go of her . . . or the meme of her dimwittedness.

Palin, to be sure, has helped stoke the meme. It would be dishonest to deny that. She doesn't think well on her feet—"All of them" was a ridiculous response to Katie Couric's innocuous but legitimate question about which newspapers and magazines Palin reads; she also mangles English syntax on a regular basis—"I want to help clean up the state that is so sorry today of journalism" is one of many Yoda-like examples.

But there has also been a genuine *gotcha* quality to much of Palin's press coverage ever since John McCain tapped her as his running mate. The tone was set in her first major network interview, with Charlie Gibson of ABC News, who asked Palin, "Do you agree with the Bush Doctrine?" Her response—"In what respect, Charlie?"—was altogether appropriate since "the Bush Doctrine" could refer to at least three ideas: (1) that spreading democracy is in America's long-term national security interests; (2) that nations who assist or give sanctuary to international terrorists are themselves guilty of terrorism; (3) that America will act preemptively if necessary to ensure our immediate security against terrorist attacks.

But instead of clarifying the question, as common courtesy required, and as he assuredly would have done for a more seasoned politician, Gibson—who apparently had only the third meaning in mind—went straight for the *gotcha*: "What do you interpret it to be . . . the Bush Doctrine enunciated September 2002, before the Iraq War?" As soon as Palin began to blather about Bush's determination to rid the world of Islamic extremism, Gibson had bagged his trophy. He had his Kodak moment.

From that moment on, the liberal media has dissected every public utterance made by Palin, right down to the last syllable, trolling for the slightest blunder or blooper or stammer. So when Palin goofs up and says, "Obviously, we've got to stand with our North Korean allies," the clip gets more airplay than the latest release from Lady Gaga. You have to wonder how the late senator Ted "fired the shirt heard round the world" and "Osama bin Osama Obama Obama" Kennedy would have stood up to such scrutiny.

Bill Maher, as I recall, never once called Kennedy a "category five moron" or a "dumb twat." Of course, after he used the latter phrase to describe Palin, the National Organization for Women immediately rallied to her defense: "If you think someone's an idiot or a danger to the country, feel free to say so, but try to keep their sex out of it."

Even if she's a dumb twat, in other words, let's say so in another way.

You have to wonder why Palin—who, I reiterate, has never held a national office, either elected or appointed—drives liberals batty. To answer that question, I'll need to slide on my special mind-reading goggles and peer into the conscious and unconscious thoughts of people with whom I disagree, to indulge in dime-store psychologizing, to treat hunches as facts and to set aside evidentiary standards and every pretense of analytical decency. In short, I'll need to write like Frank Rich. This is no easy task. Maybe if I were a theater critic Peter Principled into the realm of political discourse, I'd feel more comfortable foreshortening the critical process to a series of thumbs-up or thumbs-down rhetorical gestures; instead I've developed the inconvenient habit of substantiating what I say, grounding inference in specific observation, and keeping broad generalizations to a minimum. For now, though, good-bye to all that.

Rich rules.

So how do liberals feel about Sarah Palin? (Mind-reading goggles now in place.) To say that they hate her is too simplistic. Liberals' feelings toward Palin are more complex, an amalgam of fascination, loathing and fear that, in another context, would resemble penis envy. That sounds paradoxical, especially juxtaposed

with Maher's "dumb twat" crack. But Palin's got the kind of political mojo that causes liberals to lie awake at night and mutter
to themselves.

Much of their obsession is surely tied to her appearance, her
physical beauty. The liberal consensus is that even though Palin
lacks substance, she sparkles. She's like the shiniest glass trinket
in the window of a Times Square gift shop; only an absolute
rube, an out-of-towner who doesn't know better, would give her
a second look.

Which is precisely why she's terrifying.

For all their intellectual airs, liberals, in the damp, drizzly
Novembers of their souls, understand that they are utterly dependent on the stupid vote—that is, the votes of stupid people.
This reality underlies much of the rhetoric of the left. "Raise taxes
on the rich!" and "Make corporations pay their fair share!" are
the kinds of slogans stupid people like. They have exclamation
points, so they're easy to yell into the phone, which is especially
satisfying when you've been calling C-SPAN for years and finally
get through. Stupid people, of course, don't understand (and will
never understand) the difference between tax *rates* and tax *revenues*. They don't understand that if you *raise* tax rates you might
actually *lower* tax revenues, and vice versa. It's not that stupid
people can't do basic math; they know that if I make a million
dollars per year, and the government taxes me at 33 percent, the
government winds up with $330,000. But stupid people assume
that if the government suddenly decides to tax me at 90 percent,
it will therefore wind up with $900,000; they assume that rais-
ing the tax rate will not change my behavior, that I won't seek
out ways to shelter my money from the new tax rate, or that I

won't say to myself, "Hey, you know, now might be a good time to consider early retirement," and then move to Costa Rica to live off my savings.

Likewise, stupid people—and liberal politicians who cater to stupid people—assume that making corporations pay more for doing business will have no effect on their behavior. So, for example, back in the summer of 2010, when the Dodd-Frank Wall Street Reform and Consumer Protection Act was signed into law, Senator Dick Durbin of Illinois attached what seemed like a minor amendment reducing and limiting the "swipe fees" large banks could charge to customers who use debit cards. The difference amounted to pennies per transaction, but the cost to the banks would be billions of dollars per year. That was dandy with Durbin—who'd searched his conscience and decided that bank profits were too high.

The Durbin swipe fee caps took effect October 1, 2011... whereupon Bank of America announced it would now be charging customers who use debit cards a five-dollar monthly fee. SunTrust Banks also announced a five-dollar fee, and Wells Fargo added a three-dollar fee. Durbin was dumbfounded (though "stupefied" might be the more accurate word) and apoplectic at Bank of America's reaction, but you'd like to think a United States senator would have a basic grasp of how capitalism works: When you make doing business more expensive, businesses pass on the cost to their customers.[4]

But that's not what stupid people want to hear. They want to stick it to the rich and successful. Stupid people, in other words, are suckers for *populism*. If you want to rile up a stupid person, you just have to remind him that other people have more than he does. More money. More stuff. More influence. More leisure time. More health care. Stupid people think of economics as a zero-sum game, like a bunch of guys playing poker on a Friday night; if Bill Gates is up $60 billion, six other people must be down $10 billion each . . . and he must be cheating. That's how the *haves* screw the *have-nots*. Point out to a stupid person that he's a *have-not*—you can send him a video text message if he's not picking up his home e-mail—and that you need his help to take back the country from the *haves*, and you can count on his vote in the next election.

Not every liberal is stupid, of course, and not every stupid person is a liberal. But stupid people vote for liberal politicians in hugely disproportionate numbers. The rubber-hits-the-road giveaway—or, to continue the poker metaphor, the "tell"—is the fact that liberal politicians howl in outrage at any measure that requires voters to fill out registration forms or present identification or read instructions. They know where their bread is buttered. They know that their demographic is much more likely to screw up the process—to check off two candidates here, to leave a chad hanging there, or to forget their driver's license in their other pants. (Nor is English proficiency the issue; if even 5 percent of voting-age citizens in a district aren't fluent in English, the Voting Rights Act requires that ballots and election materials be printed in other languages. There's just no way to translate English into Stupid.) The ideal election, from a liberal perspective, is one in which the voter staggers into the voting booth and belches into a mental Breathalyzer, at which point the machine determines his electoral preferences.

What terrifies liberals about Sarah Palin, again, is that she sparkles. Stupid people are attracted to sparkly things. If a Mitt Romney or a Newt Gingrich talks about the necessity of cutting the tax rates on small businesses to stimulate job growth, stupid people tune him out. But if Palin makes the same point, and throws in a couple of populist lines about taking back our country from the media elites and Wall Street fat cats, stupid people sit up on their hind legs. They're drawn to the shiny object. They turn up the sound on their TVs. They discover she's plainspoken. She says what she means, even if it doesn't always come out right . . .

And that's the nightmare scenario for liberals: stupid people listening to a conservative. No liberal candidate can win a national election without carrying the stupid vote by a wide margin. If the stupid vote ever begins to migrate rightward in substantial numbers, the entire liberal agenda—from wealth redistribution and socialized medicine to environmental fascism and cultural relativism—is utterly doomed.

If she ever again runs for national office, Palin has the potential to put forward a smart, nuanced conservative agenda while attracting legions of stupid voters. That prospect makes her Freddy Krueger in lipstick, at least from a liberal perspective.

"The Teabaggers Creed: We're Stupid, We're Angry and It's Obama's Fault"

The term *teabagger* derives from the slang expression for a particular kind of sex act. I'd go into details, but most Americans, including many elderly and more than a few minors, now know the etymology because liberal commentators tend to revert to their name-calling, towel-snapping, high-school-locker-room selves when confronted with causes they dislike. *Teabaggers* is what passes for wit on the left. What's the equivalent on the right? I don't recall a conservative talk radio host referring to the Lesbian-

Gay-Bisexual-Transgender movement as Dykes, Fags, Freaks and Miscreants.

The Tea Party, in the minds of its political opponents, consists of equal parts stupidity, anger and hatred for President Obama . . . which itself is nothing more than thinly disguised bigotry. That's the bumper sticker formulation, the running joke wherever liberals gather to celebrate their empathy and tolerance. The truth, however, is inconvenient. For example, an April 2010 poll by the *New York Times* and CBS News found that the average Tea Party member was better educated than the average American.[5] But what about anger? Surely the Tea Party is full of rage and disdain toward those less fortunate! Except it turns out that people who don't want the federal government to redistribute wealth (read: Tea Party members) give significantly more of their personal income to charity than do the knee-jerk redistribution-ists on the left.[6]

Since the charges of knuckle dragging and foaming at the mouth are difficult to make stick, liberals tend to fall back on bigotry to explain the existence of the Tea Party. To many liberals, the belief that Tea Party opposition to President Obama's agenda is fueled by racism is unshakable. Thus, for example, in October 2009, actress-comedienne (sort of) Janeane Garofalo declared on Bill Maher's HBO program, "It's obvious to anyone who has eyes in this country that the teabaggers, the 9/12-ers, these separatist groups that pretend it's about policy—they are clearly white iden-tity movements. They are clearly white power movements. What they don't like about the president is that he's black."[7] Given the lack of corroborating evidence that followed, the words *obvious* and *clearly* could almost be read as ironic, but Garofalo was dead serious. As she continued, she was interrupted several times by rounds of applause from the studio audience.

Garofalo's analysis is by no means exceptional. They echo those of former president Jimmy Carter, who in September 2009 asserted that "an overwhelming portion of the intensely demonstrated animosity toward President Barack Obama is based on the fact that he is a black man, that he's African American . . . and I think it's bubbled up to the surface because of the belief among many white people, not just in the South but around the country, that African Americans are not qualified to lead this great country."[8]

Now Carter is in his late eighties and doddering, and Garofalo is full of the raging certainty of a C-SPAN caller. But how do you write off the fact that as she delivered her rant, her fellow Maher panelist, *New York Times* columnist Thomas Friedman, could be seen nodding in agreement? Indeed, the notion that racism is fueling resistance to President Obama's agenda has become a virtual truism on the op-ed page of the *Times*, with variations on the theme sounded by Maureen Dowd, Paul Krugman, Frank Rich and Bob Herbert. When pressed for evidence, they, like all liberals, fall back on a few allegedly racist signs seen at Tea Party rallies: "Homey don't play dat," "Long legged mack daddy," "When his lips move, he's lying," and the obligatory Obama-equals-Hitler Photoshops.

Even if you think these are indeed coded expressions of racial animus, rather than inarticulate expressions of anti-Obama sentiment, would they meet the burden of proof for the initial allegation—that the movement itself is substantially racist?

Not even close.

What's going on here is liberal commentators reasoning backward. They begin with a conclusion—the idea that many conservatives are die-hard racists—and hunt down anomalies as evidence. Their methodology is no more valid than biblical literalists who stumble across a few scraps of ancient driftwood on a hillside and shout, "Eureka, Noah's Ark!"

Liberals, as a rule, don't like to talk about evidentiary standards and logical methodology. They prefer memories and impressions—which are decidedly fallible but fine if you're trying to prove that your granny's apple cobbler is better than store-bought. On the other hand, memories and impressions rarely meet the burden of proof expected in political analysis. That's another expression liberals don't like, *the burden of proof.* It's the standard of evidence reasonably required to support an argumentative point. The reason liberals don't like to acknowledge the burden of proof is practical. The more provocative the allegation, the higher the burden of proof. In his famous critique of alien abduction stories and UFO sightings, the astronomer Carl Sagan succinctly summed up the principle: "Extraordinary claims require extraordinary evidence."[9]

Despite liberal contentions to the contrary, the charge of widespread racism among the Tea Party faithful ranks as an extraordinary claim—especially since the movement rose to electoral prominence not to contest Barack Obama's candidacy in 2008 but only after he was elected and began rolling out his policy initiatives in late 2009 and early 2010.

It's the agenda, stupid.

If you want to understand what makes a teabagger gag, consider the Health Care Summit. On February 25, 2010, at the height of the national debate over health-care reform, President Obama invited members of Congress to the Blair House to discuss the issue. The gathering was televised, which allowed politicians from both sides of the aisle to voice their expectations and concerns in public before the final legislation was crafted. The meeting should have been scored not by the Congressional Budget Office but by violins and cellos.[10]

The president set the tone for the Democrats in his opening remarks as he recalled his older daughter Malia's sudden asthma attack and his younger daughter Sasha's bout of meningitis—and how he'd wondered, both times, as he sat in the hospital emergency room, what would've happened if he hadn't had adequate insurance coverage . . .

Obama's recollections opened the floodgates, and afterward the sob stories came fast and furious: Representative Nancy Pelosi (D-CA) told of a man from Michigan whose medical bills for his bedridden wife might cause him to sell his home because he was too proud to ask his grown children for help, and of a woman from the same state whose insurance deductible was going to come out of her family's food budget. Senator Harry Reid (D-NV) then recounted the hardships of a young restaurant owner in Nevada whose daughter was born with a cleft palate; her surgeries weren't covered by his insurance policy, leaving him $90,000 in debt. Next came Representative Steny Hoyer (D-MD) with the story of an uninsured acquaintance of his who was diagnosed with a tumor; she and her working-class husband had to shell out $25,000 for her operation.

Representative Jim Clyburn (D-SC) mentioned his encounter that morning with a C-SPAN caller who was about to have transplant surgery but was told Medicare would only cover three years of postoperative treatment. Clyburn was one-upped by Representative Louise Slaughter (D-NY), who claimed that a constituent of hers was forced, presumably by lack of insurance, to wear her dead sister's dentures. "Do you ever believe," Slaughter asked, "that in America that's where we would be?" (It should be noted that Medicaid covers dentures in New York.) Senator Tom Harkin (D-IA) then whipped out a letter from a farmer whose health insurance premiums were about to rise 14 percent, putting his farm business at risk.

Senator Jay Rockefeller (D-WV) chimed in with the story of an eight-year-old boy with leukemia whose insurance ran out. "And then he died," Rockefeller stated, "because there was no insurance. Could they have cured his cancer? I don't know, but that's what insurance is for." Next up was Representative Henry Waxman (D-CA), who told of another eight-year-old boy, this one with a hole in his heart, which would be classified as a preexisting condition if his mother changed insurance carriers, so she was locked into a policy that cost her almost as much per month as her mortgage payment. Senator Dick Durbin (D-IL) then declared that he was against caps on malpractice lawsuits against doctors . . . which actually might lower the cost of medical treatment and thus insurance premiums. Such limits, he insisted, would impact a constituent of his whose face was scarred during surgery when her oxygen mask caught fire. "Are you saying that this innocent woman is only entitled to two hundred and fifty thousand dollars in pain and suffering? I don't think it's fair!"

It was left to Senator Patty Murray (D-WA) to jerk the last tear by recounting the plight of an eleven-year-old boy whose single mom got sick, lost her job, lost her health coverage—and therefore "couldn't get in to see a doctor" and died. (Again, however, not a word about Medicaid eligibility.)

The liberal politicians who came to the Health Care Summit that morning did not represent the entire Democratic Party. But they represented the vast Pity Party wing of the Democratic Party. Pity Partiers believe that the primary function of government is to right wrongs. To heal physical and psychological wounds. To redress grievances. To level outcomes. As I said at the outset, liberals prize equality over every other value. But people cannot be equal, according to Pity Party logic, until they're made whole. Hence a government that doesn't make its people whole is not doing its job. That, in a nutshell, is the mind-set of the Pity Party.

The ascendancy of the Tea Party should be understood as the intellectual and political response to the excesses of the Pity Party. The struggle between them is, in a deeper sense, a result of the basic tension between liberty and equality. Americans prize both liberty and equality; it's in our cultural DNA to do so. The problem is that liberty and equality pull in opposite directions. The more fully people are allowed the liberty to capitalize on their natural abilities, which are never evenly distributed, the more surely a hierarchy will emerge that undermines equality; some people will pull ahead as others fall behind, with accumulated advantages and disadvantages passed down from generation to generation. Inequality is inevitable in a free society. The freer the society, the more unequal it becomes. The only way to slow down that process is to prevent people from fully capitalizing on their natural abilities—in other words, to curtail their liberty. Think of it this way: The children of Conrad Hilton and Lionel Richie are born with resources and influence most other kids will never be able to match. They're born with a leg up. Should we therefore curtail the liberty of Hilton and Richie to provide that edge for their families? If we do, what's their incentive to excel? Would we be a better society if we stifled the excellence of a Hilton or a Richie?

But why should Paris Hilton (Conrad's great-granddaughter) or Nicole Richie (Lionel's adopted daughter) be riding around in limos and jetting off to Monaco? Why should they wind up with a reality TV series, which allows them to spin their pointless celebrity into lucrative business ventures of their own? What did they do to deserve any of it?

The answer, of course, is nothing. But the talents and efforts of their parents, grandparents and great-grandparents put them in an advantageous position to mass-market themselves. Sure, you end up with bad television, cheesy fashion and insufferable memoirs. Such is the cost of allowing Conrad Hilton and Lionel Richie to push their own limits, to strive against the odds, to capitalize on their innate gifts and to pass along the assets they accrue to their descendants. *That's* America. You work hard and sacrifice to give your kids a leg up.

But the idea that *anyone's* kid should be born with a leg up is offensive to the Pity Party . . . if your kid's got a leg up, he must be stepping on poor people! How can poor people live decent lives when your kid is standing on their throats? If your kid would get his damn foot off the throats of poor people, they might earn a high school equivalency diploma . . . and then they could find an executive position that doesn't require showing up early, or staying late, or reading, writing and doing stuff with numbers. Then they wouldn't have to rely on their backup plan of waking up at noon and playing lotto.

Whenever liberals talk about making the rich pay their "fair share," what they mean by the phrase is "however much of their wealth needs to be confiscated and redistributed so that no one's kid will be born with a leg up." Liberals, of course, don't see this as an attack on liberty; they see it as "spreading the wealth around"—to use one of President Obama's favorite expressions. They see it as a way to pursue equal outcomes.

It's not wrong for liberals to point out that many hardworking Americans are struggling to make ends meet. Working hard is supposed to pay off. You'd have to be an ogre not to be moved by the Pity Party examples cited at the Health Care Summit. Such stories should humble us, should make us grateful for what we have—even as we recognize their exceptional nature. But the conclusion that the government needs to wade in doesn't follow. Indeed, if the last half century has taught us nothing else, it's taught us that grand government programs designed to relieve one set of hardships tend to create another set of hardships. The Patient Protection and Affordable Care Act—the dénouement of President Obama's Health Care Summit—will surely be one such program. It's too soon to start collecting tales of woe, but it's not too hard to imagine them, the future victims of Obamacare: The father of four who dies of a cerebral hemorrhage—he thought he only had a bad sinus infection—because his primary-care doctor was too backlogged with new patients to see him for a month. The retiree forced to eat cat food as her premiums rise because younger, healthier people, knowing they can't be turned down, put off buying insurance until they desperately need it. The single mom laid off because her employer wants to keep his company under fifty workers—since any business with more than fifty workers will be compelled, as of 2014, to offer a government-approved health plan.

Who will hold *their* pity party?

The Tea Party coalesced around the principle that it is not the proper role of government to dry one person's tears by taking another person's tissues. The issue is broader than the down-on-their-luck cases recounted at the Health Care Summit. The issue is how agitated Americans should get about unequal outcomes. Our collective commitment to individual liberty means that some people will be born with the proverbial silver spoon in their mouth and others will be born behind the proverbial eight ball.

Saying that, however, it must also be noted that being born behind the eight ball in America is not exactly like waking up in a bivouac next to Dante.[11] For example, according to the Residential Energy Consumption Survey of 2005 (the last year for which data are available), 99.6 percent of poor Americans have a refrigerator— which means, in effect, that if you have a roof over your head, you have a place to store fresh food. (Oh, and if you *don't* have a roof over your head, you very likely have a mental illness or a chemical dependency that causes you to prefer to sleep on the streets rather than seek adequate shelter; the homeless are decidedly *not* like the rest of us, despite the insistence of the Pity Party, since the rest of us, if we found ourselves homeless, would sign up for the subsidized housing provided in cities across the country.) Roughly 98 percent of poor Americans have at least one television set, 65 percent at least two, 32 percent at least three, 18 percent of poor people have a wide-screen TV and 65 percent have cable or satellite connections. Eighty-one percent of poor people have a microwave oven. Seventy-eight percent live in air-conditioned homes . . . and among the 22 percent who don't, how many live in places like Bangor, Maine, or Juneau, Alaska? Sixty-two percent have a clothes washer and 53 percent a dryer, luxuries often unavailable in $3,000-per-month

Manhattan rentals. Sixty-five percent of poor people have DVD players, 55 percent have cell phones and 38 percent have home computers. Twenty-nine percent have Internet service—a number that has almost surely risen since 2005—and in case their Internet service is a tad slow, not to worry, because 49 percent also have coffeemakers to calm their nerves.[12]

As for the big-ticket items, 46 percent of poor families own their own homes—which, on average, have three bedrooms, one and a half baths, a garage and either a porch or patio. (Remarkably, the typical poor American has more living space than the typical *nonpoor* European, including residents of major cities such as London, Paris, Vienna and Athens.) Seventy-three percent of poor Americans own a car or truck, and 30 percent own two or more cars or trucks.[13]

But what about the children! Won't someone think of the children! As it turns out, the lives of America's impoverished children are not quite as Dickensian as the Pity Party would have us imagine. Not a chimney sweep in sight. Fifty-four percent of poor families with children have a video gaming system. So when they get bored with surfing the Web, texting their friends and catching the latest cable flicks, the kiddies can head over to their friend's house, kick back and disembowel one another's avatars on PlayStation.[14]

Indeed, you can argue that being born behind the eight ball in American is like being born with a silver spoon elsewhere. And that spoon gets a workout. As the comedian Chris Rock once said, "In America, we have poor people, but our poor people are fat. We don't have no fly-on-the-lip poor people." The joke is too painful to laugh at. If you're impoverished in the United States, you're *more likely* than the rest of the population to be clinically obese. Not because healthier foods cost more, and not because healthier foods are unavailable in poor neighborhoods—which Pity Partiers would realize if they'd ever spent more than five minutes in an actual poor neighborhood. Poor people are fat for the same reason they're poor: They've never learned how to delay gratification or moderate their lifestyles. That's the truth of the matter, and it's a big, fat, ugly truth. Poor people like greasy, fatty and sweet foods, so they chow down on greasy, fatty and sweet foods. They don't much like fruits and vegetables and exercise, so they avoid fruits and vegetables and exercise. They live moment to moment, doing what feels good, and not doing what doesn't feel good. The true hedonists in America are not the idle rich but the perpetually poor. They eat too much, drink too much, lie around the house too much, smoke too much, complain too much, feel sorry for themselves too much, work too little, fuck too often and with too many partners . . . and that just covers the years through high school.

Can a government substantially improve the prospects of poor people? If it's a totalitarian government, maybe. But a government dedicated to the preservation of individual liberty cannot prevent people from screwing up their own lives. It can provide a minimal safety net for their occasional strolls off the socioeconomic cliff. But it can't keep them from reflexively dangling their feet over the edge. Responsible adulthood cannot be legislated. The effort to do so bankrupts the people, morally. It bankrupts the government, fiscally.

That bankrupting effort lies at the heart of modern American liberalism.

Liberals view the Tea Party as a conservative movement because it stands in direct opposition to their hopey-changey Pity

Party sociopolitical agenda. But the Tea Party is conservative only insofar as it seeks to conserve the economic viability of the United States—which is irreconcilable with that hopey-changey Pity Party agenda. Because liberals imagine themselves as the Great White Guardians of the Historically Oppressed, they naturally conclude that whoever contests their agenda must be not only droolingly stupid and vein-poppingly angry but also irredeemably racist.

It's a conclusion rooted in bumper sticker logic.

8

=== ☆ ===

Bits and Pieces

A Miscellany of Misconceptions

> " 'War settles nothing.'
> —Dwight D. Eisenhower"

"We cannot change the hearts of those people of the South, but we can make war so terrible . . . and make them so sick of war that generations will pass away before they again appeal to it."
—William Tecumseh Sherman

> " 'Activism is the rent we pay
> for living on this planet.'
> —Alice Walker"

"One of the enduring comedies of American life is the notion that criticism of the American government is a species of heroism."
—Leon Wieseltier

"Teachers Are Not the Enemy."

. . . unless you're an inner-city child.

"I'm Already Against the Next War"

. . . Neville Chamberlain, 1938?

"Make Art, Not War"

. . . it'll confuse the heck out of Sun Tzu.

"Jesus, the Original Liberal"

. . . except for that whole religion thing.

"Jesus Scorned Hypocrites, Not Sinners!"

. . . I guess that dustup with the money changers was just a misunderstanding.

"Silly Republicans, Medicare *Is* Socialized Medicine."

. . . that's right, and bankrupting the country.

"Combine Capitalism with Socialism & We All Win"

. . . every racehorse needs an albatross.

"Socialism Is Just Government Serving the Popular Will"

. . . so let's clamp down on the media and round up the clergy.

"The GOP Stands for Organized Money and Expensive Wars"

. . . wait, wouldn't that make it the OMEW?

"We Are Who We've Been Waiting For"

. . . let's hope we get here soon because my feet are killing me.

"How Can You Oppose Universal Health Care and Be Pro-Life?"

. . . how can you oppose discrimination and be pro-choice?

"Seriously, the Founding Fathers Were Pro-Choice"

. . . not sure their slaves would agree.

"I Think, Therefore I Am a Democrat"

. . . *Cogito, ergo* jackass?

"Liberalism Is What Happens When You Stop & Think"

. . . shouldn't that be "stop thinking"?

"We Are a Nation of Immigrants"

. . . the wait-your-turn, law-abiding kind.

"Somos Una Nación de Inmigrantes"

. . . *que aprendió a hablar inglès.*

"Don't You Dare Call Me Unpatriotic!"

. . . how about "perversely loyal"?

"New Racism Is No Better Than Old Racism"

. . . affirmative action versus slavery, hmmm.

"Hatred Is Not a Family Value"

. . . could've fooled Marvin Gaye.

"Lack of Health Care Kills More
Americans Than Guns Do"

. . . so if an intruder climbs through your window,
cough on him.

"Taxes Buy Civilization"

. . . which makes *Jersey Shore* the most civilized place
on earth, right, Snooki?

"Why Do So Few Have So Much of Our Wealth?"

. . . why do rock stars have so much of our sex?

"Isn't It Blasphemous to Use Religion to Get Elected?"

. . . not if you know the definition of the word *blasphemous*.

"Most Secularists Are Also People of Faith"

. . . waiting on a Venn diagram for this one.

"I'm a Christian *and* a Democrat"

. . . still waiting on that Venn diagram.

" 'Religion is what keeps the poor from murdering the rich.' —Napoleon"

. . . if we could only get rid of that pesky sixth commandment!

"Don't Pray in My School, and I Won't Think in Your Church"

. . . don't sketch in my bathroom,
and I won't piss in your art gallery.

"Doing My Part to Piss Off the Religious Right"

: . . psst, Copernicus, no one's paying attention.

"God Is Just Pretend"

. . . so let's stop kidding ourselves about unalienable rights.

"The Most Common Form of Terrorism in the USA Is That Carried Out by Bulldozers and Chainsaws"

. . . but the trees started it by occupying holy logging land!

"The Bridge to the 21st Century Is Shovel-Ready"

. . . but we can't build it because spotted owls
live near the riverbank.

"Use It Up, Wear It Out, Make It Do, or Do Without"

. . . sounds like tree-hugger marriage advice.

"Without Nature, There Is No Food or Shelter"

. . . but at least there's still clothing, right?

"Fossil Fuel Is Dead"

. . . the only good allosaurus is the one powering your Volvo.

"Poverty Is the Greatest Threat to the Institution of Marriage"

. . . and having children outside of marriage is
the greatest cause of poverty.

"History. Civics. Math. Is There ANY Class the Teabaggers Didn't FAIL?"

. . . hygiene. Now let's talk about the Wall Street Occupiers.

"Right-Wing Radio Makes You Dumb & Mean"

. . . but at least it pays for itself. Now let's talk about NPR.

"Whatever Rush Says, Believe the Opposite"

. . . but what if Rush tells us to trust bumper stickers?

"I Stand with the 99%"

. . . official motto of the Coalition of Pastured Sheep.

"The Whole World Is Watching"

. . . on devices made by multinational corporations.

"Labor Creates Wealth. Wealth Does Not Create Labor."

. . . tell that to the guy making my flat-screen TV.

"No One Is Free When Others Are Oppressed"

. . . *phew*, that's a load off my mind!

"There's a Reason Why GREED Is a DEADLY SIN"

. . . there's a reason why SLOTH is one also.

"Whenever You Concentrate Wealth & Power, the Gangsters Move In"

. . . quote from *A People's History of Hip-Hop?*

"Being Homeless Is Not a Crime"

. . . at least not until you urinate on the sidewalk.

"Well-Behaved Women Rarely Make History"

. . . celebrate the legacy of Roseanne Barr.

"I'm a Sexy, Smart, Pro-Choice, Democratic Woman!"

. . . and doggone it, people like me!

"Smart, Sexy & Liberal"

. . . two out of three ain't bad.

"Abraham Lincoln Was Our Most Liberal President"

. . . before or after he suspended habeas corpus?

"Silence Enables Tyranny"

. . . watch out for that mute button on the remote!

"Diversity Without Division"

. . . without division, what does diversity look like?

"The Death Penalty Deters Nothing"

. . . but it cuts down significantly on recidivism.

"Apathy Is a WMD"

. . . which is why I never let bomb-sniffing dogs near my crotch.

"An Eye for an Eye Makes the Whole World Blind"

. . . the Gospel according to Moe?

"Terrorism Has No Country or Religion"

. . . but it does have a two-word catchphrase.

"Dare to Think for Yourself"

. . . yeah, dude, listen to the bumper sticker!

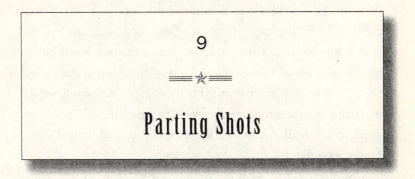

Absolutes, Occupiers and Olive Branches

Another thought experiment, the last one: Suppose you're a photo-journalist working for, say, *National Geographic.* Your editor Nigel calls you into his office for your next assignment. He tells you about a tribe of Aborigines recently discovered on a remote tract of land in the outback of Australia. He wants you to do a photo essay. Nigel hands you a manila envelope. Inside the envelope is a round-trip plane ticket, the name of your local guide and a fact sheet on what's currently known about the Kwakkwak tribe. As you are about to leave the office, Nigel drapes his arm over your shoulder and says, "Get me good pictures."

Early the next morning, you climb aboard Qantas Airways for the twenty-four-hour flight to Sydney. After takeoff, you settle into your first-class seat and glance, for the first time, at the fact sheet on the Kwakkwaks. You find details on their agricultural methods, their hunting rituals and their social customs. As you read to the bottom of the page, you notice that the Kwakkwaks practice polygamy. You, of course, having grown up in the United States, having grown accustomed to monogamy, reflexively regard marriage as an arrangement between two people. Still, you don't think much about it. You set aside the fact sheet and hunker down for the long flight.

It's already afternoon of the following day when the plane touches down in Sydney. You meet up at the airport with your contact, Rod Laver (not the tennis player), claim your knapsack and climb into a waiting taxi. You and Rod Laver ride for hours and hours, the countryside becoming more and more remote, until the last paved road ends. Then you and Rod Laver climb out, and he leads you to a pair of bicycles he's hidden behind a boulder. The two of you pedal along ever more treacherous dirt roads until nightfall, then camp out and stash the bikes, rise at dawn and hike for fourteen hours until at last, just before another sunset, you drag yourself into the village of the Kwakkwaks. There is a ceremony taking place. Rod Laver nudges you and explains that the son of the Kwakkwak chief is about to marry three village women—ages nineteen, seventeen and fifteen.

You feel a wave of nausea at the sight. Suddenly, the fact that the tribe is polygamous is more than just a footnote; the reality of three women, the youngest one only fifteen years old, marrying the same man strikes you as plain wrong. You feel inside your knapsack for your safety revolver. You *can* stop the ceremony; it's within your power.

But do you have the moral right to do it?

Now you and I are creatures of Western civilization, not to mention cable TV reruns, so we've cut our teeth on *Star Trek*'s Prime Directive—the principle that a more technologically advanced culture must not interfere with the natural development of a more primitive culture. That's the liberal ethos of the 1960s in a nutshell. So of course we know what to do in this situation. Live and let live, right? Tolerance is the sign of an intellectually evolved human being. *No way* does an outsider, such as yourself, have the moral right to stop that ceremony. You don't want to wind up in Captain Kirk's intergalactic doghouse. Besides, who are you to judge? Doesn't Hamlet warn his buddies Rosencrantz and Guildenstern, "There is nothing either good or bad, but thinking makes it so"?[1] That settles it. You bite your tongue, hang around the tribe for a few more days, snap your photos, write your essay and by the end of the week, you're back in New York City, sliding the photos and text across the desk to Nigel.

All right, you're halfway through the thought experiment.

Nigel is pleased with the job you've done. He's so pleased, as a matter of fact, that he's got another assignment for you. While you were gone, he explains, another tribe of Aborigines was discovered, the Gleekgleeks. Nigel wants you to do another photo essay, and you want to keep Nigel smiling, so you nod your head, and he slides another manila envelope across the desk. "Look," he says, leaning back in his chair, "I know you had a hard time with that polygamy business. You'll be glad to know the Gleekgleeks are as monogamous as you and I."

By the next morning you're back aboard a Qantas jet, out over the ocean, on your way to Sydney. You're scanning down the fact sheet on the Gleekgleeks. Their agricultural methods, hunting rituals and social customs seem much like those of the Kwak-kwaks; for a moment, you're filled with apprehension . . . but then, toward the bottom of the page, you note that the Gleekgleeks are indeed monogamous. You feel relieved. But your relief turns to horror a moment later as you notice the very last line of the fact sheet:

The Gleekgleeks practice human sacrifice.

But there's no turning back now. The afternoon of the follow-ing day, your jet touches down in Sydney. You meet up with Rod Laver again, claim your knapsack and climb into a waiting taxi. You ride hours and hours until the last paved road ends. Then you bicycle for hours until nightfall, make camp for the night, then hike for another day until at last you stagger into the village of the Gleekgleeks. There is a ritual taking place. Rod Laver explains that a three-month-old baby girl is about to be dismembered in order to appease tribal gods. Your guts seize up. Again, you feel inside your knapsack for your safety revolver. You *can* stop the ritual; it's within your power.

But do you have the moral right?

The question isn't as straightforward now, is it? You've got two irreconcilable principles tugging at your conscience. On the one hand, there's the Prime Directive. The Gleekgleeks have evolved a culture very alien to ours, just as the Kwakkwaks have. Don't both tribes have a right—in fact, an equal right—to decide what's right and wrong *for them?* On the other hand, there's your natural instinct to protect the innocent. Surely, it's wrong to stand by and watch a baby slaughtered. If *anything* is wrong, that's wrong. Come to think of it, when Hamlet lectures his buddies on the relativity of good and evil, isn't he pretending to be crazy?

So what do you do?

I've presented this thought experiment to hundreds of people in the last decade—friends and family, colleagues and students. The majority of them, you may be amazed to hear, have decided that the Prime Directive trumps the instinct to protect the innocent. They'd let the baby girl die. Perhaps you yourself have come to that conclusion. If so, congratulations, you've just constructed a powerful defense of the South's position on slaveholding during the Civil War. Oh, and you've also cast a vote to acquit the Nazi leaders on trial at Nuremberg after World War II. If every society has an unlimited right to decide for itself what's right and wrong, then the abolitionist movement in the North had no moral standing to condemn, let alone to undermine, the institution of slavery in the southern states; Lincoln was not the Great Emancipator but a narrow-minded bully. And if every society has an unlimited right to decide for itself what's right and wrong, then the Nuremberg prosecutors had no moral standing to try Nazi leaders for "crimes against humanity"—since the defendants had worked within the laws of the Third Reich.

But if you elected to rescue the baby girl, if you felt reason and decency *compelled* you to rescue the baby girl, then you just crossed a significant intellectual threshold. Welcome to Judgmental Junction, the first stop on the train of thought that leads to conservatism. For once you intervene in the sacrifice of the baby girl, you're saying, in effect, that what the Gleekgleeks regard as morally right is in fact morally wrong. You're saying that laws made by human beings must be judged against higher laws—since it would be ridiculous to say that Gleekgleek laws are morally wrong simply because they're different from the laws you're familiar with. Indeed, the fact that you were willing to tolerate polygamy among the Kwakkwaks but not child sacrifice among the Gleekgleeks illustrates the point that difference, in itself, does not equate with wrongness.

But of course saying that human laws must be judged against higher laws presupposes that "higher laws" exist—which is the baseline insight shared by every conservative. That doesn't mean that conservatives always agree on the content of those higher laws or on their application in different circumstances. (Starting from the premise that higher laws exist, I've written columns in favor of legalizing gay marriage and upholding *Roe v. Wade*, positions at odds with a majority of conservative commentators.) But at least conservatives reason outward, from first principles toward policies.

Liberal policies, by contrast, tend to be more of a grab bag of immediate, and often fleeting, interests—the kind of interests that run as deep as bumper sticker slogans. They fade over time, and in the sunlight of debate, but so what? You can always scrape them off and paste on new ones. In an unintentionally revealing *Washington Post* column, written after George W. Bush defeated John Kerry in the 2004 presidential election, the liberal critic Michael Kinsley bemoaned the fact that Americans now live in the "Disunited States."[2]

> We on my side of the great divide don't, for the most part, believe that our values are direct orders from God. We don't claim that they are immutable and beyond argument. We are, if anything, crippled by reason and open-mindedness, by a desire to persuade rather than insist. Which philosophy is more elitist? Which is more contemptuous of people who disagree?

As an exercise in navel-gazing, Kinsley's passage calls to mind Jesse Ventura's notorious pronouncement in a *Playboy* interview that organized religion is "a crutch for weak-minded people,"[3] or maybe, going even further back, Allen Ginsberg's passionate declaration in the opening of the poem *Howl* that he's seen the "best minds of [his] generation destroyed by madness." Such statements always tell you more about the mind-set of the intended audience than about the actual state of things. Just as a typical *Playboy* reader would regard churchgoers as superstitious hayseeds, denying themselves pleasures of the flesh out of an irrational attachment to fairy tales, and just as a typical 1950s bohemian would identify doped-up poets buzzing around the Greenwich Village, rather than physics geeks pulverizing atoms at Princeton, as the true geniuses of his era—likewise, a typical twenty-first-century liberal holds an exceedingly warped view of the relative reasonableness of liberals versus conservatives.

Conservatives may or may not believe that their values are "direct orders from God"—as Kinsley claims. But they do believe that certain principles are "immutable and beyond argument." Or, as Thomas Jefferson put it, "self-evident." That's the reason conservatives have no problem with the Gleekgleek predicament; they'll save the baby every time. From a conservative perspective, the polygamous Kwakkwaks are the more problematic tribe. Conservatives tolerate differences, indeed celebrate differences, but if the third bride at that wedding is only fifteen years old . . .

Conservatives, in short, are judgmental.[4] They're at ease with the existence of absolutes, intellectual and moral yardsticks, lines that cannot be crossed. Not every conservative recognizes exactly the same lines, of course. But they take for granted that the lines are out there, dividing truth from falsehood, right from wrong, tolerable from intolerable.

Crossing such lines is, from a liberal perspective, an act of courage. That's the reason "transgressive" is such a high compliment in liberal-speak. It means you're willing to take on the status quo, to stick your thumb in the eye of tradition, to flip conservatives the bird as you zip past them on life's interstate. As for absolutes, liberals reject them out of hand. They have to. If intellectual and moral yardsticks exist, then some wise guy is going to start using them to measure stuff. And you know where that leads, don't you? Ranking. That guy's smarter than that guy. That kind of family works better than that kind. That society is more just than that one. If your goal in life is to level things, you can't acknowledge the existence of absolutes. Absolutes are anathema.

That would make a decent bumper sticker, come to think of it: *Absolutes are anathema*. It's concise. It's rhythmic. It's even got alliteration. Then again, it's also polysyllabic and requires a moment or two of thought, so it might not work. It might even be a hazard. You won't want lightbulbs clicking on over liberals' heads while they're cruising down Route 80.

Still, liberals are fun to have around. The world would be a far duller place without liberals because they're far more willing than conservatives to make total jackasses of themselves. As I write these words, hundreds of unwashed, unfocused, attention-starved young people, urged on by a drum circle of graying, ponytailed, crypto-Marxist refugees from the sixties, are "occupying" Wall Street, protesting corporate capitalism, documenting their ersatz revolution on iPhones, iPads and MacBooks.

Give 'em a year or so with the Dalai Lama and they might achieve callow.

But the Occupy Wall Street movement, in its sophomoric contradictions, is a pitch-perfect microcosm of modern liberalism. As the columnist Mark Steyn has noted, "They're anarchists for statism, wild free-spirited youth demanding more and more government control of every aspect of life—just so long as it respects the fundamental human right to sloth."[5] George Will's take on the movement's message is even more succinct: "Washington is grotesquely corrupt and insufficiently powerful."[6]

There is no intellectual coherence among the Occupiers, only an idée fixe: inequality. They cannot bear the fact that American-style capitalism results in wildly unequal outcomes. That's their observation. That's also their entire argument, though to call it an argument is to misrepresent it. It's more of a self-righteous grunt, a narcissistic demand to be heard despite an inability to form meaningful sentences. What do they want? *It's not fair, man.* What's not fair? *You know, it . . . everything. Banks. Corporations. America.* If you keep asking questions, though, you can deduce an underlying principle: The purpose of the government, in their minds, is to shrink the gap between the *haves* and *have-nots*. It's job one. Even if America's *have-nots*, when compared with a majority of residents of the planet, would be counted among the *haves*. If you follow the reasoning of the Occupiers, the Congo's the place to be because the entire nation is dirt poor. No one's got a leg up on anyone else—at least not for very long since roving machete squads will hack off a leg at a moment's notice. But who knows? If just the right warlord comes to power, with just the right grasp of central planning, maybe the government can provide the entire population with crutches . . .

But let me end with an olive branch. Or, if not quite an olive branch, at least an outstretched hand for the occasional straw men

I've trotted out and knocked down over the last hundred or so pages:

Not only are liberals fun to have around, but they're also intermittently useful. Given the perennial tension between liberty and equality, and the fact that conservatives tend to subordinate the latter to the former,[7] you *need* a consistent voice for equality to keep things on a relatively even keel. You might not think it's the government's job to tell the CEO of a bank how much money he can make—even if the bank has just been bailed out by the government—but if the guy decides to take his full hundred-million-dollar compensation package, do you really want him to feel okay about it? He deserves to be shamed, to glance out the window of his corner office and see a protester or two on the street below. Which is where liberals come in. You think conservatives are going to paint slogans on their body parts and march around in the cold? Conservatism needs a rhetorical counterweight, even if the rhetoric is logically gelatinous.

That's liberalism's conservative function.

Notes

Sticker Shock: By Way of an Introduction

1. "KU Helps Bumper Stickers Stick Around," *Topeka Capital-Journal*, February 14, 2011, http://cjonline.com/news/state/2011-02-14/ku-helps-bumper -stickers-stick-around#.TxD2MGNrMyA.
2. Thomas Frank, *What's the Matter with Kansas?* (New York: Metropolitan Books, 2004).

1: Race to the Bottom

1. The desire to recruit greater numbers of black and Hispanic students has an unspoken corollary, which runs something like this: "You know, we've got too many Jews and Asians around here . . . we've got to get rid of some of them." It doesn't make for much of a rallying cry, but it's the unavoidable flip side of the quest for "diversity"—as evidenced by the fact that Asian students now occasionally refuse to identify their ethnicity on their college applications. See, for example, "Some Asians' College Strategy: Don't Check 'Asian,'" *USA Today,* December 3, 2011, http://www.usatoday.com/news/education/ story/2011-12-03/asian-students-college-applications/51620236/1.
2. Richard H. Sander, "A Systematic Analysis of Affirmative Action in American Law Schools," *Stanford Law Review*, November 2004, http://www.law .berkeley.edu/faculty/rubinfeldd/SanderFINAL.pdf.

3. "Anti-Semitism and Prejudice in America," Anti-Defamation League, http://www.adl.org/antisemitism_survey/survey_iii.asp.

4. The historical relationship between race and regulation in the financial sector is fraught with ironies. Liberals currently demand tighter regulation of the banking industry, including its lending practices—which liberals deem "predatory." But the more tightly the government regulates the lending practices of banks, the less flexible banks can be in making loans. The less flexible banks can be in making loans, the more they will have to turn down potential borrowers who do not meet precise risk and collateral formulas, a disproportionate number of whom are certain to be black borrowers. But if banks turn down black borrowers in disproportionate numbers, liberal advocacy groups like the NAACP will charge them with racism. Liberal politicians, in turn, will demand that lending regulations be relaxed . . . around and around we go.

5. Dayo Olopade, "Skip Gates Speaks," *Root*, July 21, 2009, http://www.theroot.com/views/skip-gates-speaks?page=0,1.

6. A copy of the official police report is available online here: http://www.samefacts.com/archives/Police%20report%20on%20Gates%20arrest.PDF.

7. Peter Nicholas, "Obama Calls Comments on Cambridge Police Poor Choice of Words," *Los Angeles Times*, July 25, 2009, http://articles.latimes.com/2009/jul/25/nation/na-obama-gates25.

8. Peter Wallsten and Mike Dorning, "Obama Cheers a 'Teachable Moment' Over Beer with Gates, Crowley," *Los Angeles Times*, July 31, 2009, http://articles.latimes.com/2009/jul/31/nation/na-beer-summit31.

9. *Wonders of the African World with Henry Louis Gates, Jr.*, http://www.pbs.org/wonders/.

10. Alessandra Stanley, "Genealogy for a Nation of Immigrants," *New York Times*, February 9, 2010, http://www.nytimes.com/2010/02/10/arts/television/10faces.html.

11. Cornel West, "Niggerization," *Atlantic*, November 2007, http://www.theatlantic.com/magazine/archive/2007/11/niggerization/6285/.

12. Touré, *Who's Afraid of Post-Blackness?* (New York: Free Press, 2011), 121.

13. The category "colored," it should be noted, also included American Indians.

14. The "one-drop rule" is an example of *hypodescent*, which the anthropologist Conrad P. Kottack describes as a classification scheme that "automatically assigns the children of a mixed union or mating between members of different socioeconomic groups in the less privileged group." See Conrad P. Kottack, "Human Diversity and 'Race,'" *McGraw Hill Online Learning Center*, http://highered.mcgraw-hill.com/sites/0072500506/student_view0/chapter5/faqs.html.

15. Sir Charles Linné, *A General System of Nature*, trans. William Turton (London: Lackington, Allen, 1806), 9. (Original: Carl Linnaeus, *Systema Naturae*, 1767.)

16. Ibid.

17. Johann Friedrich Blumenbach, *The Anthropological Treatises*, trans. Thomas Bendyshe (London: Longman, Green, Longman, Roberts & Green, 1865), 264–76.

18. Quoted by Bruce Baum, *The Rise and Fall of the Caucasian Race* (New York: New York University Press, 2006), 81.

19. Quoted by Lance Morrow, "The Provocative Professor," *Time*, June 24, 2001, http://www.time.com/time/magazine/article/0,9171,157721,00.html.

20. Quoted by Massimo Calabresi, "Dispatches Skin Deep 101," *Time*, February 14, 1994, http://www.time.com/time/magazine/article/0,9171,980105,00.html.

21. Paul R. Gross and Norman Levitt, *Higher Superstition: The Academic Left and Its Quarrels with Science* (Baltimore: Johns Hopkins University Press, 1998), 203–14.

22. James Davison Hunter, *The Death of Character: Moral Education in an Age Without Good or Evil* (New York: Basic Books, 2000), 269–72.

23. Alan Charles Kors and Harvey Silvergate, *The Shadow University: The Betrayal of Liberty on America's Campuses* (New York: Free Press, 1998), 193–209. For a more recent and sympathetic note on the subject, consider Linda Lum, "A Space of Their Own: Ethnic-Themed Dorms Offer a Supportive Environment for Minorities, but Critics Say They Stunt Personal Growth by Promoting Self-Segregation," *Diverse Issues in Higher Education,* December 11, 2008, http://findarticles.com/p/articles/mi_m0WMX/is_22_25/ai_n31165417/?tag=content;col1.

24. Kors and Silvergate, *The Shadow University*, 193–209.

2: Dogma and Denial

1. Ronald Bailey, "DDT, Eggshells, and Me," *Reason*, January 7, 2004, http://reason.com/archives/2004/01/07/ddt-eggshells-and-me.

2. Malcolm Gladwell, "Mosquito Killer," *New Yorker*, July 2, 2001, http://www.gladwell.com/2001/2001_07_02_a_ddt.htm.

3. Michael Finkel, "Malaria," *National Geographic*, July 2007, http://ngm.nationalgeographic.com/2007/07/malaria/finkel-text.

4. National Oceanic and Atmospheric Association, U.S. Department of Commerce, "Trends in Atmospheric Carbon Dioxide," http://www.esrl.noaa.gov/gmd/ccgg/trends/.

5. "Last Time Carbon Levels Were This High: 15 Million Years Ago, Scientists Report," *ScienceDaily.com,* October 8, 2009, http://www.sciencedaily.com/releases/2009/10/091008152242.htm.

6. Steve Connor, "Global Growth in Carbon Emissions Is 'Out of Control,'" *Independent*," November 11, 2006, http://www.independent.co.uk/environment/climate-change/global-growth-in-carbon-emissions-is-out-of-control-423822.html.

7. Fareed Zakaria, "How Will We Fuel the Future?," review of *The Quest: Energy, Security, and the Remaking of the Modern World*, by Daniel Yergin, *New York Times*, September 23, 2011, http://www.nytimes.com/2011/09/25/books/review/the-quest-by-daniel-yergin-book-review.html?_r=1&pagewanted=all.

8. Carbon emissions figures come from the Millennium Development Goals Indicators site of the United Nations Statistics Division. Data can be found at http://mdgs.un.org/unsd/mdg/SeriesDetail.aspx?srid=749.

9. John DeCicco and Freda Fung, "Global Warming on the Road: The Climate Impact of America's Automobiles," *Environmental Defense*, 2006, iv–viii, http://www.edf.org/sites/default/files/5301_Globalwarmingontheroad_0.pdf.

10. Robert Vale and Brenda Vale, *Time to Eat the Dog?: The Real Guide to Sustainable Living* (London: Thames & Hudson, 2009).

11. "The Carbon 'Pawprint' of Pets," *RedOrbit.com,* December 22, 2009, http://www.redorbit.com/news/science/1802592/the_carbon_pawprint_of_pets.

12. Sarah Netter, "Authors Claim Pets Are More Damaging to Environment Than SUVs," ABC News, December 23, 2009, http://abcnews.go.com/Technology/pet-dogs-damaging-environment-suvs/story?id=9402234#.TsGBIoA4Mbc.

13. No one reveres Jefferson's writings more than I do, but the notion that every word that dripped from his pen is sacrosanct is foolish. Consider that in response to the (admittedly outrageous) Alien and Sedition Acts of 1798, he authored the Kentucky Resolutions, which argued that states had the right to nullify federal laws: "Resolved: That the several States composing, the United States of America, are not united on the principle of unlimited submission to their general government; but that, by a compact under the style and title of a Constitution for the United States, and of amendments thereto, they constituted a general government for special purposes—delegated to that government certain definite powers, reserving, each State to itself, the residuary mass of right to their own self-government; and that whensoever the general government assumes undelegated powers, its acts are unauthoritative, void, and of no force: that to this compact each State acceded as a State, and is an integral part, its co-States forming, as to itself, the other party: that the government created by this compact was not made the exclusive or final judge of the extent of the powers delegated to itself; since that would have made its discretion, and not the Constitution, the measure of its powers; but that, as in all other cases of compact among powers having no common judge, each party has an equal right to judge for itself, as well of infractions as of the mode and measure of redress."

14. Mark Goldblatt, "Liberty, Logic and Abortion," *Philosophy Now,* June/July 2002. The essay contains a critical analysis of *Roe v. Wade*. It is available online at the *PN* website and mirrored here: http://markgoldblatt.com/2011/08/liberty-logic-and-abortion.html.

3: War and Peace

1. Quick aside on Maher, who's made a lucrative career of mocking religious belief: It's a fallacy to think that his show or his studio audience is any more cerebral than Jerry Springer's. The fact that the former focuses on national politics while the latter focuses on sexual infidelity doesn't raise the level of debate. "Puh-leeze!" is not one whit more logically decisive than "Yeah, well fuck you!"

2. Quoted by Tom Rockmore, *Before and After 9/11: A Philosophical Examination of Globalization, Terror, and History* (New York: Continuum, 2011), 98.

3. The Osama-Qutb connection has been well documented. Osama's mentor and cojihadist, Ayman Zawahiri, was a student and follower of Qutb; while studying at King Abdulaziz University, Osama attended weekly lectures by Qutb's brother, and fellow students recall Osama as deeply drawn to Qutb's thought.

4. The suggestion that America's foreign policy is to blame for Islamic militancy and terrorism is of course taken quite seriously by many liberals who oppose American foreign policy. The problem is how to account for, let's say, the 1989 Iranian fatwa on the writer Salman Rushdie; the 2001 dynamiting of ancient statues of Buddha by the Taliban in Afghanistan; the 2002 Miss World riots in Nigeria, which left more than two hundred dead; the 2004 murder of Dutch filmmaker Theo Van Gogh in Amsterdam; the 2005 Danish cartoon riots in several countries, which left more than one hundred dead; etc. Each incident was a response not to colonialism or imperialism but to a perceived affront to Islam and to Muslim sensibilities.

5. Al Baker and William K. Rashbaum, "Police Find Car Bomb in Times Square," *New York Times*, May 1, 2010, http://www.nytimes.com/2010/05/02/nyregion/02timessquare.html.

6. Ibid.

7. Amanda Ripley, "The Fort Dix Conspiracy," *Time*, December 6, 2007, http://www.time.com/time/magazine/article/0,9171,1692025,00.html.

8. Mark Goldblatt, "The Ultimate WMD," *American Spectator Online*, August 7, 2007, http://spectator.org/archives/2007/08/07/the-ultimate-wmd.

9. Ibid.

10. Ibid.

4: Hero Worship

1. Norman Mailer, "The White Negro," *Dissent*, Fall 1957, http://www.dissentmagazine.org/online.php?id=26.

2. Gross and Levitt, *Higher Superstition*, 107–48.

3. Quoted by Jonah Goldberg, *Liberal Fascism: The Secret History of the American Left from Mussolini to the Politics of Meaning* (New York: Doubleday, 2007), 273.

4. Ibid.

5. Stephanie Schriock, "Twenty Years Later, Anita Hill's Fight Is Still Ours," *Huffington Post*, October 11, 2011, http://www.huffingtonpost.com/stephanie -schriock/anita-hill_b_1005689.html.

5: Bush Derangement Syndrome

1. Florida Supreme Court chief justice C. J. Wells correctly predicted that the U.S. Supreme Court would have to intervene once the majority of Florida justices granted Gore's request to continue selective hand-recounts beyond the legal deadlines stipulated by Florida law: "I could not more strongly disagree with their decision to . . . prolong this judicial process. I also believe that the majority's decision cannot withstand the scrutiny which will certainly immediately follow under the United States Consti-tution. . . . My succinct conclusion is that the majority's decision has no foundation in the law of Florida as it existed on November 7, 2000, or at any time until the issuance of this opinion. The majority returns the case to the circuit court for this partial recount of under-votes on the basis of unknown or, at best, ambiguous standards with authority to obtain help from others, the credentials, qualifications, and objectivity of whom are totally unknown. That is but a first glance at the imponderable problems the majority creates. . . . Importantly to me, I have a deep and abiding concern that the prolonging of judicial process in this counting contest propels this country and this state into an unprecedented and unnecessary constitutional crisis. I have to conclude that there is a real and present likelihood that this constitutional crisis will do substantial damage to our country, our state, and to this Court as an institution."

2. In assessing Bush's decision to oust Saddam, you might also take into ac-count the following statement from former Russian president Vladimir Putin—who opposed the invasion of Iraq—reported by CNN on June 18, 2004: "I can confirm that after the events of September 11, 2001, and up to the military operation in Iraq, Russian special services and Russian intelligence several times received . . . information that official organs of Saddam's regime were preparing terrorist acts on the territory of the United States and beyond its borders, at US military and civilian loca-tions." Putin passed along the information to Bush. See "Russia 'warned U.S. about Saddam,'" http://articles.cnn.com/2004-06-18/world/russia .warning_1_russian-special-services-president-vladimir-putin-russian -intelligence?_s=PM:WORLD.

3. Matt Welch, "The Politics of Dead Children," *Reason*, March 2002, http:// reason.com/archives/2002/03/01/the-politics-of-dead-children.

4. Rich Lowry, "The Case for the 'Torture Memos,'" *National Review Online*, April 21, 2009, http://www.nationalreview.com/articles/227334/case-torture -memos/rich-lowry.

5. The Yoo-Bybee "torture memo" may be read in its entirety here: http://www .uchastings.edu/faculty-administration/faculty/paul/class-website/docs/ BybeeTortureMemo.pdf.

6. "President Bush's Speech on Terrorism (transcript)," *New York Times*, September 6, 2006, http://www.nytimes.com/2006/09/06/washington/06bush_transcript. html?pagewanted=all.

7. Mark Danner, "Tales from Torture's Dark World," *New York Times*, March 14, 2009, http://www.nytimes.com/2009/03/15/opinion/15danner.html?pagewanted=all.

8. Ibid.

9. David Stout, "White House Releases Documents Related to Prison Abuse," *New York Times*, June 22, 2004, http://www.nytimes.com/2004/06/22/politics/22CND -ABUS.html.

6: The Commonweal and the Government Teat

1. Mark Goldblatt, "Alec Baldwin, Right on Taxes," *American Spectator Online*, March 6, 2009, http://spectator.org/archives/2009/03/06/alec-baldwin-right -on-taxes.

2. City of New York Mayor's Office of Film, Theatre and Broadcasting, "How the Tax Credit Works," http://www.nyc.gov/html/film/html/incentives/tax _credit_overview.shtml.

3. The theory behind the "Laffer Curve" was neither discovered nor named by Arthur Laffer, as he himself has explained. See Arthur Laffer, "The Laffer Curve: Past, Present, and Future," Heritage Foundation, June 1, 2004, http:// www.heritage.org/research/reports/2004/06/the-laffer-curve-past-present -and-future.

4. Quoted by Charles Krauthammer, "Return of the Real Obama," *Washington Post*, September 22, 2011, http://www.washingtonpost.com/opinions/return -of-the-real-obama/2011/09/22/gIQAf7dsoK_story.html.

5. David Logan, "Summary of Latest Federal Income Tax Data," Tax Founda- tion, October 24, 2011, http://www.taxfoundation.org/news/show/250.html.

6. Hannah Roberts, "Stinking Up Wall Street: Protesters Accused of Living in Filth as Shocking Pictures Show One Demonstrator Defecating on a Police Car," *Daily Mail*, October 19, 2011, http://www.dailymail.co.uk/news /article-2046586/Occupy-Wall-Street-Shocking-photos-protester-defecating -POLICE-CAR.html.

7. Logan, "Summary of Latest Federal Income Tax Data."

8. Ibid.

9. The Congressional Budget Office lists the federal budget deficit for 2010 as $1,294,000,000,000.

10. Data can be found at the Internal Revenue Service website. See "Selected Income and Tax Items, by Size and Accumulated Size of Adjusted Gross Income, Tax Year 2009" (Table 1.1).

11. One of the more disturbing questions swirling about the Patient Protection and Affordable Care Act (aka "Obamacare") is the extent to which insurance providers under the plan will have to cover psychotherapy. Obamacare contains a provision for mental health parity. While still a U.S. senator in 2007, Obama explained that mental health parity "means that we don't allow group health plans to impose treatment or financial limitations on mental health benefits that are different from those applied to medical or surgical services." But parity opens a very big can of worms, if for no other reason than that Obama has stressed the crucial role of "prevention" in improving health care. Since physical ailments ranging from hypertension and ulcers to acne and sexual impotence have psychological components, and since more severe mental ailments often flow from less severe ones, wouldn't Obama's commitment to prevention suggest that psychotherapy must likewise be covered? The trouble with *that*, however, is that there's no scholarly consensus about what its goals are, what its proper methodology consists of, or whether it works better than just ordinary social interaction. If Freudian psychoanalysis and Gestalt therapy are covered, does that mean that art therapy or dance therapy or primal scream therapy must also be covered? Beyond these lie other dilemmas that future secretaries of health and human services will likely confront. If psychotherapy can reduce or prevent certain physical and mental illnesses, cannot the same be said of meditation? What about aura cleansing? Crystal healing? Will future secretaries, armed with the Obamacare mandate for mental health parity, and committed to preventive medicine, say no to *anything*?

12. In addition to his Ironshrink blog, Smith also writes regularly for *Psychology Today*. He has frequently demolished pseudoscientific attacks on conservatism. See "Are Liberals More Intelligent than Conservatives? Another Broken Study Says It Is So," Ironshrink.com, April 7, 2010, http://ironshrink.com/2010/04/are-liberals-more-intelligent-than-conservatives-another-broken-study-says-it-is-so.

13. Paul Taylor, "Republicans: Still Happy Campers," Pew Research Center, October 23, 2008, http://pewresearch.org/pubs/1005/republicans-happier.

14. S. E. Cupp and Brett Joshpe, *Why You're Wrong About the Right* (New York: Threshold Editions, 2008), 112.

15. Jaime L. Napier and John Jost, "Why Are Conservatives Happier Than Liberals?," *Psychological Science* 19:6 (2008): 571, http://www.psych.nyu.edu

/jost/Napier%20&%20Jost%20(2008)%20Why%20are%20conservatives%20
happier%20than%20libe.pdf.

16. George Will, "Bleeding Hearts but Tight Fists," *Washington Post,* March 27, 2008, http://www.washingtonpost.com/wp-dyn/content/article/2008/03/26/AR2008032602916.html.

17. U.S. Department of Health and Human Services, Administration for Children and Families, Office of Planning, Research and Evaluation, *Head Start Impact Study Final Report,* January 2010, http://journalistsresource.org/wp-content/uploads/2011/08/1108HeadStartImpact.pdf.

18. Jens Ludwig and Deborah Phillips, "The Benefits and Costs of Head Start," *National Bureau of Economic Research* (2007): 5, http://www.nber.org/papers/w12973.pdf.

19. Ron Haskins, "Getting Ahead in America," *National Affairs,* Fall 2009, http://www.nationalaffairs.com/publications/detail/getting-ahead-in-america.

20. Eleanor Chute, "In High Schools, a 'B' Is New 'C,'" *Pittsburgh Post-Gazette,* June 3, 2007, http://www.post-gazette.com/pg/07154/791202-298.stm.

21. Volumes have been written on the rationale for the opposition of teachers' unions to merit pay initiatives. For a recent summary see Megan McArdle, "How Unions Work," *Atlantic,* February 4, 2010, http://www.theatlantic.com/business/archive/2010/02/how-unions-work/35327.

22. William Bradford, *Of Plymouth Plantation* (1623), available at http://press-pubs.uchicago.edu/founders/documents/v1ch16s1.html.

23. Or perhaps liberals' aversion is not to human nature per se but to the fact that it is not malleable. The permanence of human nature is the central insight of Freud. It's the central error of Marx.

24. "Drug and Alcohol Abuse and the Homeless," AddictionBlog.org, January 7, 2011, http://alcohol.addictionblog.org/drug-and-alcohol-abuse-and-the-homeless.

25. Cited by Nancy Kennedy, "Path to a New Beginning," *Citrus County Chronicle Online,* October 25, 2008, http://www.chronicleonline.com/content/path-new-beginning.

26. In fact, the 1996 National Survey of Homeless Assistance Providers and Clients found that exactly 66 percent of the homeless population had mental illnesses and/or drug or alcohol addictions. There is no reason to think the percentage has changed dramatically in the last decade and a half.

27. "One Third of Americans One Paycheck Away from Homelessness," *Naked Capitalism,* October 5, 2011, http://www.nakedcapitalism.com/2011/10/one-third-of-americans-one-paycheck-away-from-homelessness.html.

28. Heather Mac Donald, "Advocates of Excuses," *New York Post,* February 1, 2002, http://www.manhattan-institute.org/html/_nypost-advocates.htm.

29. Ibid.

30. Ibid.

31. You can take the bum off the street, but you can't take the street out of the bum. The textbook illustration of this, of course, is the case of Joyce Patricia Brown—also known as "Billie Boggs"—who occupied a street grating on East Sixty-Fifth Street for about a year in the mid-1980s. Drug-addled and demented, Brown spent her waking hours cursing at neighborhood residents, ranting and mumbling incoherently, ripping up, burning and urinating on dollar bills she collected from passersby, smearing herself with feces and occasionally darting into traffic on Second Avenue. On October 28, 1987, she was forcibly removed, institutionalized and medicated under a program initiated by Mayor Ed Koch . . . at which point the New York Civil Liberties Union sued for her release. The case became a cause célèbre. Finally, a liberal judge ruled that she couldn't be held against her will or forced to take her medications. Upon her release, Boggs was cleaned up and interviewed by Phil Donohue and Regis Philbin; she was invited to deliver a lecture at Harvard Law School on the plight of the homeless. As soon as her celebrity died down, however, she went off her meds and fell back into her former life. She wound up living on the streets again, screaming at pedestrians, soiling herself and mumbling incoherently. When her sudden fall from grace was pointed out to Mayor Koch, his response was "Shock! Shock!"

7: Bêtes Noires

1. Jeff Jacoby, "Abandoning Gaza Won't End Terrorism," *Boston Globe,* May 6, 2004, http://www.boston.com/news/globe/editorial_opinion/oped/articles/2004/05/06/abandoning_gaza_wont_end_terrorism?pg=full.

2. Ibid. As absurd as it is to suggest that Israeli policies caused the cold-blooded murder of a pregnant woman and her children by Palestinian gunmen at close range, Jacoby points out that that was the actual position taken by National Public Radio reporter Julie McCarthy.

3. Many of the Palestinians had fled their homes inside Israel—or been expelled by Jews, depending on whose history you trust—in the years leading up to the 1948 war.

4. The monthly swipe fees were eventually scrapped after Durbin took to the floor of Congress to denounce Bank of America. But BOA and the rest have since added miscellaneous service charges to make up for the lost revenues. See Richard Burnett, "Banks Roll Out New Fees After Debit Fees Fail to Fly," *Baltimore Sun,* February 18, 2012, http://www.baltimoresun.com/business/os-banks-new-stealth-fees-20120218,0,1928258.story.

5. Kate Zernike and Megan Thee-Brenan, "Poll Finds Tea Party Backers Wealthier and More Educated," *New York Times,* April 14, 2010, http://www.nytimes.com/2010/04/15/us/politics/15poll.html?pagewanted=all.

6. Arthur Brooks, "Tea Partiers and the Spirit of Giving," *Wall Street Journal*, December 24, 2010, http://online.wsj.com/article/SB10001424052748704774604 576036010174911064.html.

7. *Real Time with Bill Maher*, October 2, 2009. The full text and video of Garofalo's rant can be found at http://newsbusters.org/blogs/brent-baker/2009/10/03 /garofalo-led-limbaugh-tea-baggers-white-power-movement-motivated -racism.

8. Ewen MacAskill, "Jimmy Carter: Animosity Towards Barack Obama Is Due to Racism," *Guardian*, September 16, 2009, http://www.guardian.co.uk /world/2009/sep/16/jimmy-carter-racism-barack-obama.

9. "Carl Sagan on Alien Abduction," interview with NOVA, February 27, 1996, http://www.pbs.org/wgbh/nova/space/sagan-alien-abduction.html.

10. "Health Care Summit (full transcript)," *CNN.com*, February 25, 2010, http:// transcripts.cnn.com/TRANSCRIPTS/1002/25/se.03.html.

11. The poverty statistics that follow are based on the pre-2011 definition used by the U.S. Census Bureau, which is based on a family's cash income relative to purchasing power; it's deceptive because it doesn't take into account government assistance, which can add thousands of dollars per year to a family's purchasing power. In November 2011, the Census Bureau rolled out an alternative measure of poverty favored by the Obama administration—and, based on the new measure, declared that the ranks of the poor had risen by three million to a record high of forty-nine million. The new measure, designed to supplement but not replace the old, is perhaps even more deceptive because it pegs the threshold for poverty not to purchasing power but to the overall income of Americans. As Robert Rector and Rachel Sheffield—coauthors of *Understanding Poverty in the United States*—point out, according to the new measure of poverty, if the incomes of all Americans magically doubled overnight, with no corresponding inflation, the number of poor people would remain unchanged because the poverty thresholds would have doubled as well. The only way to reduce poverty, by the newer measure, is to level the incomes of Americans.

12. Robert Rector and Rachel Sheffield, "Air Conditioning, Cable TV, and an Xbox: What Is Poverty in the United States Today?," Heritage Foundation, July 19, 2011, http://www.heritage.org/research/reports/2011/07/what -is-poverty.

13. Ibid.

14. Ibid.

9: Parting Shots

1. William Shakespeare, *Hamlet*, edited by Willard Farnham (New York: Penguin Books, 1986), 2.2.250–51. References are to act, scene and line.

2. Michael Kinsley, "Am I Blue?," *Washington Post*, November 5, 2004, http://www.washingtonpost.com/ac2/wp-dyn/A29470-2004Nov5?language=printer.

3. Ventura's interview with *Playboy* appeared in the November 1999 issue.

4. *Judgmental* and *tolerant* are not antonyms; you can think something is wrong but still recognize the right of others to differ. You can celebrate differences, as long as the differences recognize Jefferson's self-evident truths and exist within the bounds of reason and decency.

5. Mark Steyn, "Corporate Collaborators," *National Review Online*, November 6, 2011, http://www.nationalreview.com/articles/282280/corporate-collaborators-mark-steyn.

6. George F. Will, "Can Occupy Wall Street Give Progressives a Life?," *Washington Post*, October 12, 2011, http://www.washingtonpost.com/opinions/can-occupy-wall-street-give-liberals-a-lift/2011/10/11/gIQA8GyCgL_story.html?hpid=z3. Will's summary dismissal of the movement is a sardonic masterpiece: "OWS's defenders correctly say it represents progressivism's spirit and intellect. Because it embraces spontaneity and deplores elitism, it eschews deliberation and leadership. Hence its agenda, beyond eliminating one of the seven deadly sins (avarice), is opaque. Its meta-theory is, however, clear: Washington is grotesquely corrupt and insufficiently powerful."

7. Of course, the conservative push for greater and greater liberty is not infinite, which is the anarchist position. Nor, of course, does the push for greater and greater liberty mean that conservatives favor blanket legalizations of abortion or flag-burning or gay marriage or narcotics or pornography or prostitution, which is the libertarian position. On social issues, conservatives tend to favor the liberty of traditional communities to define their own moral standards and to enact legislation in support of those standards. But, of course, those moral standards are always circumscribed by Jefferson's self-evident truths, as well as by reason and decency.